A VOICE IN THE WILDERNESS

A Bishop's Prayer Journey through the Arabian Peninsula

John Brown

[Thus says the Lord]
I am about to do a new thing;
now it springs forth, do you not perceive it?
I will make a way in the wilderness
and rivers in the desert.

Isaiah 43:19

The conversation of brethren
should help and cheer us, but God's
voice speaks most often in silence

Father H H Kelly, SSM
Founder of the Society
of the Sacred Mission: "Principles"

The desert is an attempt to go forward,
stripped and feeble,
deprived of all human support,
fasting from all earthly and even spiritual food,
to an encounter with God

René Voillaume

This Reflection is for Rosemary my wife,
whose love, encouragement and support
have sustained me through our many travels
and upheavals for more than fifty years.
Also for the many Christians who still
persist in saying their prayers
and conversing with God day after day,
without quite knowing why.

A note about the author

John Brown was born in 1930 in Grimsby in Lincolnshire. He was trained for ordained ministry in the Anglican Church by the Society of the Sacred Mission at Kelham Theological College near Newark and was sent from there to St. George's Cathedral in East Jerusalem, (then in Jordan), where he was a boarding house master at St. George's Upper School.

Bishop John is a graduate in theology of London University and was ordained deacon and priest in Jerusalem in 1955-56. He and his wife Rosemary were married at St. George's Cathedral. He was transferred to Amman, the capital of Jordan, where he taught at Bishop's School and was also the Anglican Chaplain in Amman and East Jordan. After a spell in the UK in the aftermath of the Suez crisis he was appointed as a missionary in Northern Sudan, based in Omdurman and with a brief to prepare Arabic speaking ordinands and catechists for ministry in Khartoum/Omdurman and Kordofan in the Nuba Mountains.

When he was able to hand his work over to Sudanese people Bishop John returned to parish work in the UK where he was later appointed as Archdeacon of Berkshire in the Oxford Diocese. During his years as archdeacon he also worked as Christian coordinator of HRH Prince Hassan bin Talal's work on Christian-Muslim dialogue through the a:al al-bayt Royal Foundation centred on Amman. During these years Bishop John formed close ties with the Pontifical Institute for Arab and Islamic Studies run by the White Fathers in Rome and with the Community of St. Egidio, also based in Rome.

In 1986 Bishop John was elected Bishop of Cyprus and the Gulf, during which time he was much occupied in strengthening relationships with Muslims in the Arabian Peninsula and especially with the rulers and their ministers. He retired from his diocese in 1995 and is now Assistant Bishop in the Diocese of Lincoln.
He continues to speak on inter faith matters and to work for a better understanding between the people of the world faiths.

Contents

    Preface 6

    Foreword 7

    Map 9

    Introduction 11

1. **Iraq:**
   Setting out as the Lord bids 18

2. **Kuwait:**
   High tech. In the killing fields 33

3. **Bahrain:**
   Oil wells and palm groves 48

4. **Qatar:**
   Reality television 56

5. **The United Arab Emirates:**
   Church planting 65

6. **The Sultanate of Oman:**
   The generous land 74

7. **The Yemen Republic:**
   Arabia Felix? 86

8. **Saudi Arabia:**
   The unyielding land 97

9. **Human rights and human responsibilities** 107

10. **Christian–Muslim relations** 121

    Notes 136

    Further Reading 137

Preface

The author of this book lived in the Middle East from 1987 until 1995 when he was Bishop of Cyprus and the Gulf and had the opportunity to have a deep experience of the culture, faith and life of the region. His appeal to readers is that when we read the book we should put prejudice aside and open ourselves to the desert experience. His hope is that we will struggle to understand the minds and hearts of the people of the region who are all the children of Abraham: Jews, Christians and Muslims.

In many ways this is a practical book because it asks us not simply to read, but also to pray and through prayer to be led into the 'mind of Christ' and into action for the Middle East and its suffering people. Through reading the book we may prayerfully come to see the Middle Eastern region afresh as a place where there is much to learn and, in the words of the author, 'where it is hard to separate the human and the divine'.

Christians Aware is honoured to have the opportunity to publish this book which is very much in keeping with most of our other books. It is not academic but rather offers a wonderful insight, and through that offering there is the challenge to us the readers to change, grow and act for justice and peace in the Middle East.

Barbara J. Butler
Christians Aware 2008

Foreword

by
The Right Reverend David Hope
formerly Archbishop of York

One of the regular features of any intercessions either in private or in public worship, be they at the Eucharist or at some other service, is what is so often described in a somewhat vague way as 'the situation in the Middle East'. The person leading the prayers may then go on to be more specific, naming particular places - Iraq, Afghanistan, Israel and the Palestinian peoples, Iran and so on.

John Brown's excellent book *A Way in the Wilderness* is a plea that our prayer be informed, that we seek to pray with understanding, to enter into the sensitivities and paradoxes which any intercessory prayer poses for us all, and not least ourselves never to shirk the real struggles, questions, agonies and difficulties but rather to stay with them, often in a silent helplessness before God.

This is the context for his rich reflections on his years particularly as Bishop of Cyprus and the Gulf. He takes us with him to countries as diverse as Saudi Arabia, Oman, Yemen and the United Arab Emirates, where he speaks of 'church planting'. He seeks to disabuse us of our ingrained prejudices about such countries and with the aid of selected passages from the sacred writings of the Jewish, Muslim and Christian faiths, together with excerpts from their commentators and scholars, presents us with an altogether more rounded and knowledgeable background against which we may pray.

The journey is interwoven too with fascinating stories of the bishop's encounter not only with rulers and statesmen, but also with the ordinary people of the land, thus giving us a unique insight into how they themselves understand their own faith, life and culture, and perhaps more importantly how they perceive us. He shows how the various denominational labels and claims we as Christians divided in such a context make for ourselves become not only an irrelevance but also a veritable hindrance in the furthering of the Gospel.

It may come as a considerable surprise, for example, to discover Bishop John Brown discussing some of the finer points of the Protestant Reformation with Sheikh Saqr the ruler of the tiny sheikhdom of Ra's al Khaimeh (at the Sheikh's instigation and about which he was extremely knowledgeable).

Perhaps however the most important sections of this book are the final chapters in which John Brown draws together his immense experience, knowledge, pastoral sensitivity and not least in the context of his own deep spirituality, his reflections on human rights and responsibilities and Christian–Muslim relations.

From beginning to end this is primarily a book written with the object of helping 'Christians who are not resident in the Middle East, and especially the Arabian peninsula, to pray with more knowledge and sensitivity about Christian–Muslim relationships as they tend to be in these violent times and as they should be in settled times'. The author certainly achieves his purpose and a whole lot more too. Here is a book which cannot fail to encourage all who pray, often in unknowing and in anguish about situations and circumstances from which they are far distant. Such prayer of course can be a very risky business and those who embark upon it will find themselves being drawn the more deeply into the mystery of Christ's passion and death: that death which was for the healing of the nations and which even now still summons all who have a care for reconciliation, justice and peace in the world to an altogether more serious engagement with what can so often seem to be either impossible or intractable — for 'with God all things are possible'.

David M Hope

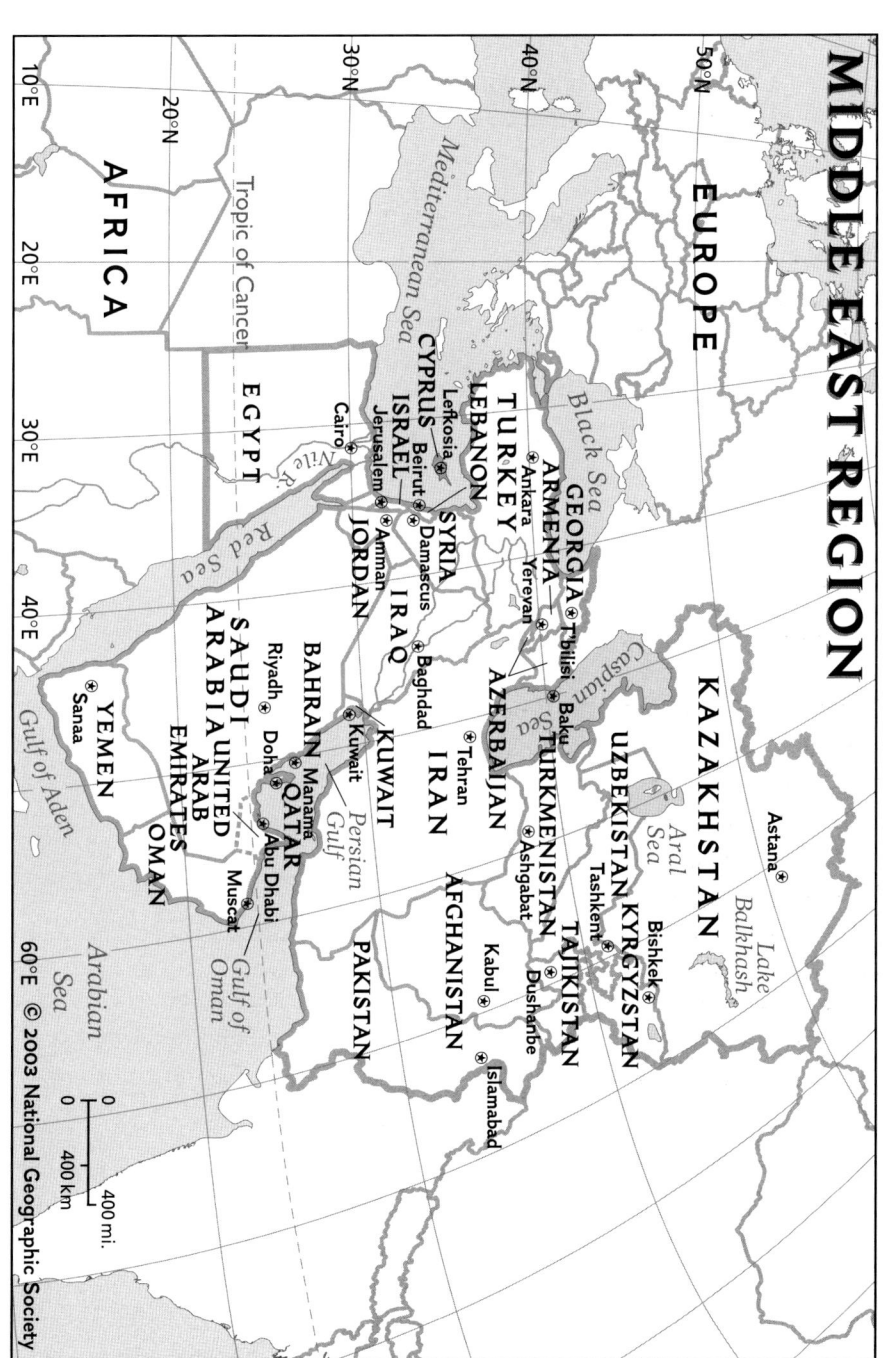

*A meeting of the synod of the diocese of Cyprus and The Gulf.
Bishop John is in the centre of the front row and on the left is Bishop Azad Marshall,
Bishop of Iran since 2007.*

Introduction

The aim of this book is to help Christian churchgoers to pray intelligently and with knowledge about Islam and the relationship between Christianity and Islam as it develops in the early years of the twenty first century. It is not written as a book for students of Islam, but as a guide as to how we might converse with God in our private and public devotions about the Middle East, the people: Jews, Christians and Muslims, who live and work there, and how they interact. The Middle East and the religions associated with it bring to the surface many of the fears and anxieties we experience, especially when we read the newspapers and watch television, and these are reflected in the way we pray and swing between panic and fatalism as we realise how much faraway events affect our daily lives; especially when they come ever closer to our own daily lives: in New York, Madrid, London and other places. The writing of this book springs from trying to answer many questions from churchgoers, usually after I have given a talk about Islam or Christian–Muslim relations; thus it is an attempt to answer pastoral need.

It has become clear to many Christians in the present age, which some call 'post-Christian' (which is not to say it is totally secularised), that prayer cannot simply be mouthing off words to an invisible yet somehow omnipotent creator in the hope that he will be able to do something miraculous about the chaotic state of the world. Yet in private prayer and public worship we cling to the belief that in some way intercessory prayer will get through to God and that he will act in accordance with our wishes; in justification of this we recall the words of Jesus: **I will do whatever you ask in my name, so that the Father may be glorified in the Son. If in my name you ask me for anything, I will do it** (John 14:13–14). Have we as Christians really thought through what Jesus of Nazareth meant when he said **Whatever you ask for in prayer with faith, you will receive** (Matthew 21:22)? Are we confident that what we ask for, either privately or at public worship, really conforms to the will of God and that we are not simply expressing our own preferences? Have we not come to understand (or at least wonder) during the agonies of the Twentieth century that if we pray to God in faith for particulars (for example, for the earthly healing of a friend or loved one from a malignant disease, our earnestness in faith may in itself be ignoring what might be God's own larger plan? The question becomes even more difficult when we pray in general terms, as in a litany or at the time of intercessory prayer during a public service. When we pray, presumably in faith, for peace in the world, for a good harvest, for justice and so on, are we praying this for ourselves alone or for the whole world? And if for the whole world, how do we take account of the many diverse cultures, faiths, value-systems, political ideologies and so on? Is there any point in asking God, through our prayers, to deal in generalities? Is he really a manipulator, a kind of control-freak? We are well accustomed in the practice of our faith to understand that God is not a magician and we believe that he cannot act against his own nature; so why does so much of our praying in faith (as we understand it) appear to expect that God will respond to our requests, when all around the world others are praying in faith, making their requests known to God, so many of which are entirely contrary to our own?

Of course, these questions have been thought about since the beginning of faith in a power beyond our own power, and it does not require great intellect to recognise that the three monotheistic faiths especially are in a state of utter confusion when it comes to working out the relationship between human beings and God himself. The confusion, however, is not merely a matter of the intellect. It is also a matter for the emotions; not simply cerebral, but visceral, and we Christians should at least recognise that it is not acceptable practice to go to church week after week, or into our private world, wherever that is, day after day, and use language to God that simply does not make sense and is an insult to our own God-given faculties and to the mind of God himself.

This little book is a pastoral attempt to discover how we, people who have faith in God, and more specifically faith in God through Jesus Christ, may begin to attain to something Paul called **the mind of Christ**

(Philippians chapter 2) and become more and more integrated into the being of God our creator father. Greek Orthodox Christians describe what I personally am seeking in my own pilgrimage as **enthewsis** or 'in-godding' and this is a spiritual pilgrimage that does not rely too much on the use of man-made language. It has more to do with attending to God in mind and spirit and what Brother Roger of Taizé called "dans le silence"; it is worth infinitely more than a struggle to find appropriate words.

Looking back now on a long life and ordained ministry I can see that I have always experienced a struggle in the background with my intercessory and petitionary praying. That is not to say I have not persisted. I think many of us wrestle with the question 'Why doesn't God do something about this or that or the other?' while at the same time persisting in prayer. There are of course plenty of stories in the New Testament, such as the 'importunate widow' or the Syro-Phoenician woman who simply asked for some crumbs of comfort, and they seem to point to the need for persistence, a determination even in moments of doubt and uncertainty to refuse to believe that God will not or cannot heed what we say or ask for. The alternative is a kind of fatalism, an underlying suspicion that for all our persistence God will in the end do what he wishes to do, but that we must in one way or another make our own needs and thoughts known to him. I discovered how this might be when I was a young priest in the Sudan. The congregation in Omdurman was made up of many young people from a diverse number of tribes who had come from the areas of traditional African religions into the city and were relative newcomers to Christianity. Their faith was strong and the Christian church in the Sudan, since the 1960s and through many years of civil war and much internal prejudice against Christians, has been vibrant, faithful and strong. Yet, whenever these young tribal Christians crowded into church for the Eucharist they came wearing charms and amulets of the kind used to ward off evil spirits and the power of the kujur, or village witch doctor. We are scarcely more sophisticated, with our superstitions and over-active imaginations as we walk the streets and avoid walking under ladders, as we throw salt over our left shoulder, as we imagine that evil is coming upon us through the malevolence of other people or the capricious behaviour of material things in the house or at work.

All these questions and paradoxes have been highlighted in my own life through spending much time working in the Middle East. Especially as I travelled around the Arabian Peninsula and discovered the awesome strength of the deserts I began to realise that I was constantly trying to work out what it was I thought I was doing in my praying. I hope that you will take up the journey with me, as I take you through places whose names have become very familiar to everyone who watches the television news.

I am sure that before I can have a conversation with God that is not merely gobbledegook I have to be completely honest within myself; that is, in my heart, mind and spirit. I have to recognise my own prejudices and work at getting rid of them, so that what my nature cries out for when I intercede with God or petition him may correspond to what God's own nature cries out for also. St Paul says that we do not know how to pray as we ought, but that God's Holy Spirit **intercedes with sighs too deep for words** (or, as in the Authorised Version, **for we know not what we should pray for as we ought: but the Spirit maketh intercession for us with groanings which cannot be uttered.** (See Ep. Romans 8:26).

Those lands and civilisations that saw the birth of religious faith in a power beyond our own earthly power, lands with which we shall be pre-occupied in this journey of discovery and prayer, were countries whose inhabitants never could easily separate the divine from the human; society lived on earth from the society that might be perceived as belonging to the supra-human. The people of the Middle East have always struggled to find a route through the empty quarters of Arabia alongside a route through the empty quarters of the mind and spirit; for Jews, Christians and Muslims alike it is a search for a way through the wilderness, and in that search faith, politics, spiritual and human longings become mixed up and are inseparable. What follows is an example of what patterns the struggle might take. Christians today have become very familiar with the Arabic word **jihad**. It means 'struggle' and is often translated in popular usage as 'holy war.' Much has been written by Muslims concerning **jihad** and many misunderstandings concerning Muslims and Islam have arisen because of un-Islamic emphases placed on this word by radical Islamists. The opening chapter beginning our prayer journey through Arabia will underline to the open hearts and minds of faithful Jews, Christians and Muslims how adherents of all three faiths are engaged in a life of prayerful dialogue with God which, because of all we are learning about the evolving world in which we live, can only be seen as a struggle and never as the enunciation of bland words to a being of our own making existing for our own desires.

I first visited Iraq in the 1980s during the war between Iran and Iraq. My first most vivid memory of Baghdad is of the many motor cars and taxis with coffins strapped to their roof racks. The coffins held the bodies of soldiers and many of the vehicles were on their way to the great mosques of Karbala and Najaf, the Shi'ite holy cities, where the bodies were taken and honoured before burial. My second vivid memory is of the great number of Volkswagon Passat cars being driven around; these were the regular gifts of Saddam Hussein to the families of young officers who had been killed in battle. Violence is never far away in the Middle East, either as a threat or an actual day-to-day reality, and Iraq has been as violent as any other Middle Eastern country in its long history.

I hope that this book will encourage and lead to prayer. It does not contain many prayers, but attempts to inform the reader's mind and heart in such a way that prayer and reflection will come accompanied by knowledge and sympathetic understanding. It is not my purpose to provide a detailed history of the countries of the Arabian Peninsula, or of Judaism, Christianity or Islam; plenty has been written about all these things, for the specialist and non-specialist, and the bibliography at the end will, I hope, encourage further reading. The history of the Christian church in the eastern Mediterranean and in the Arabian Peninsula itself goes back to apostolic times and today, because Christians live as minority groups in Muslim lands, there are many misunderstandings on the part of Christians living in nominally Christian and developed societies with regard to Judaism in Israel, eastern Christianity and the various and diverse faith interpretations and practices of Islam.

The Middle East is a part of the world where passions run high and emotions are vividly expressed. In every part of the Arab Muslim world nothing excites the passions so much as the existence of the State of Israel, and those of us who are Christians and have a deep concern for the remaining Christians in the Middle East and who regularly and frequently pray publicly and privately for the people of the Middle East need to possess the kind of intellectual integrity that is willing to put to one side ideological prejudices and lay ourselves open to the painful desert experience that will likely bring our hearts and minds closer to the mind of Christ.

John Brown

Note

Each chapter contains:

1. a brief overview of the country being discussed;
2. a personal account to aid understanding prayer;
3. some aids to meditation and reflection.

The translation of biblical texts used throughout is that of the New Revised Standard Version, except for the Psalms which are taken from *The Psalms: a historical and spiritual commentary* by John Eaton (Continuum 2005). Most of the translations from the Quran are taken from *The Quran: Arabic text with new translation* by Muhammad Zafrullah Khan, published by Curzon Press.

The transliteration of Arabic words is always a problem for writers and a matter for discussion. I have not distinguished between short and long letters and have not invented signs to show guttural letters or other orthographic signs; the only exception is that I have occasionally introduced : after a vowel in order to lengthen the vowel; for example, 'a:l'. Most of the Arabic words used will be familiar to the reader.

Chapter 1
Iraq
Setting out as the Lord bids

Let us begin with the story of Abraham, although the history of Mesopotamia, including modern Iraq, goes back much further. When I read the story of Abraham I feel I am in the presence of someone I know. It does not matter to me that scholars and archaeologists sometimes question whether there was ever a man called Abram. People like him must have lived in the rich fertile farm lands between the Tigris and the Euphrates through many millennia and we have no reason to suppose that they did not experience the same inner emotions that we experience, of joy and sorrow, of success and failure, especially in the economy; of doubt and certainty and of cynicism and wonderment.

Genesis 12 and the following chapters give a graphic account of nomadic life in what today constitutes southern Iraq, the marshlands and Ur of the Chaldeans. This is where Abram's family originated, and from there their wanderings took them through northern Iraq into the regions of modern Kurdistan, eastern Turkey and Syria, settling for a time in the wide country to the east of the northern Euphrates, near Haran in the region called Aram-Naharaim ('Aram of the two rivers'). This nomadic way of life and the wanderings of inter-related families across the deserts and mountains are replicated in the bedouin way of life today. Eventually, as we read in Genesis 24, Isaac son of Abram married Rebekah of Nahor in Aram-Naharaim. Abram ('exalted ancestor') was re-named Abraham ('ancestor of a multitude' - see NRSV note on Genesis 17:5).

Already, as we begin this prayer journey through the Arabian Peninsula, we have much on which to reflect and about which to pray. Today, especially as we fly over these vast desert lands, we need strong imaginations to take us back to Genesis 12:1–9 and Abraham's journey of faith. Sometimes, as my flight descended on its approach to a Gulf airport, we would be treated to the sight of large camel trains moving across the sands in their wonderfully rhythmic swaying motion, their Bedouin riders swaying with them.

The writer of the letter to the Hebrews tells us that **faith is the assurance of things hoped for, the conviction of things not seen** (Hebrews 11:1). Abraham was asked to have what we sometimes call 'blind faith'. Like Abraham, we often do not know where our faith will take us in life.

Instead of saying that we have faith in God and that he will show us what to do in our lives through our praying and reflecting on his word in scripture, we use phrases like 'I'll follow my star', or 'It's my destiny to go such-and-such a way'. But it is far better to acknowledge a faith in a power beyond our own power and recognise that events in the world are used by God in order to develop his evolving purposes in the world and in each one of us.

It may be that Abraham's family moved from Ur of the Chaldeans northwards because of poor harvests or lack of rain. We don't know, and cannot know, what possessed Abraham to move on from Aram-Naharaim towards the Mediterranean coastal region and into the land of Canaan; or what finally persuaded him and his family to buy land in Hebron. The reasons do not matter, for we are following the trail of a nomadic people whose lives and economy, whose social and family habits, were very different from our own; but we are able to go back to their times and reflect that with them the kind of faith which shows trust in and dependence upon a supreme being was born.

Jews, Christians and Muslims describe themselves as 'children of Abraham'. The popular view is that one of Abraham's children (Isaac) was born of Sarah, and another (Ishmael) of Hagar. The real history of the two families cannot now be known, but the traditions are important for us today. A belief that the Hebrew people descended through the Abraham/Sarah/Isaac line, while the Arab peoples descended through the line of Abraham/Hagar/Ishmael, and that these two lines are for ever destined to be enemies, can have no reasonable place in our religious beliefs or devotions. The families of Isaac and Ishmael moved along

**The Arabs call Abraham al-khaleel,
the Friend, and this is also the Arabic name
for Hebron; so we may begin
our prayer reflection by reminding ourselves
that, by the covenant made with Abraham,
God declared himself to be his friend,
so through Abraham the friend of God
we too start off as children of the
covenant, friends of God.**

their own nomadic routes, Ishmael wandering southwards into Arabia along the incense route and the Sinai Peninsula (Genesis 25:12-18) and Isaac's family moving in and out of the territory now covered by Syria, Israel/Palestine and Gaza (Genesis 25:19-26:3). No doubt the two families/tribes met up and mixed from time to time, and the two brothers came together to bury their father in Hebron (Genesis 25:9).

In the last quarter of the eighth century BCE, and in the first quarter of the sixth century, what is today modern Iraq was affected by the influx of Jewish exiles, the first group from Israel (the northern kingdom) and the second from Judah (the southern kingdom), whose lands were conquered respectively by the Assyrians and by the Chaldeans under Nebuchadnezzar.

Whenever I journeyed through Iraq in the days of Saddam Hussein I tried to pray my way to an understanding of why the fundamental tragedy of the Middle East ever happened. I began my working life as a teacher and priest in the divided Jerusalem of 1954 and was constantly reminded by my Arab pupils that the tragedy derived from the appalling and self-regarding policies and mistakes made chiefly by the British and French governments following the 1914–1918 world war, leading to the arbitrary carving up of the Arabian and Levantine countries and the eventual establishment of the State of Israel in 1947. A prayer journey of reflection and intercession requires that we try to understand the mind-set of those for whom we pray and about whom we are reflecting, in this case the children of Abraham — Jews, Christians and Muslims. Iraq, rather than Israel/Palestine, is a good place to begin such a meditation, but it is not a painless one.

The Eighth century BCE prophets make it very plain that the Jewish inhabitants of Palestine had, for all their economic stability, consistently broken covenant with God. The books of, for example, Amos, Hosea and Micah are short and it is helpful to read them slowly as part of our reflection and meditation before prayer. These prophets were deeply affected by what we would today call 'the permissive society', and by the corrupt political structures of the time, as prevalent in their day as in our own. They observed what was going on in their society and communities, interpreting the signs of the times (Amos, for example, was clearly affected by the solar eclipse of 763 BCE) and warning the people to amend their ways and restore their part of the covenant with God. The Eighth century prophets were the first of the so-called 'writing prophets' and when the calamities of exile to Mesopotamia fell upon them, especially when Judah and Jerusalem were left desolate in the Sixth century, people would be reminded of the many warnings of the prophets of the preceding two centuries So it was that the Jewish people experienced great and irretrievable loss: of home, land, family unity and all those things we all take for granted and which we regard as our human right.

It is very much part of human experience that when we suffer a sense of loss of any kind we begin to return to perhaps long-forgotten paths of faith. Individuals express great sorrow, whole communities lament, whether they are scores of thousands of Armenians in Turkey and Jews in Auschwitz-Birkenau, many thousands of Arabs displaced from their Palestinian homes and land in the late 1940s and in 1967; innocent Iraqis in Halabja killed by Saddam Hussein's lethal chemical weapons, or New Yorkers in Manhattan in September 2001. Great suffering has long been endemic in the Middle East and the recent history of Iraq demonstrates how once-great empires can be brought down, and their innocent citizens with them, through the megalomania of tyrants and the greedy territorial ambitions and desire for economic control on the part of those who collude with tyranny. It is with regard to this last observation that western Christians especially have to be guarded in their criticisms and judgements of the developing tragedy of Iraq, and learn how to pray in the full knowledge of our part in that development. This is not easy, nor is it painless. For many years the United States and Britain encouraged the Ba'athist secular regime of Iraq by supplying arms and weapons which could only lead to the destruction of entire communities; then, when Saddam Hussein became too tyrannical for the western world's own comfort, he ceased to be the western world's friend and became the terrorist. Faced with these constant contradictions in human behaviour, together with an uncritical use of language (words like 'terrorism' and 'undemocratic' are beginning to be used as synonyms for anything that is contrary to current northern and western hemisphere political policy), it is difficult to see how Christians who take prayer seriously can fail to ask political questions of themselves and of their elected representatives before trying to obtain some understanding and receive guidance from God.

There is a strong warning here not to let our praying get out of hand. Through many centuries the Jewish people have suffered a very great deal at the hands of non-Jews, and especially Christians. All through these centuries the Jews produced the most wonderful poets, musicians, political and social philosophers and artists; yet the longing for revenge, for compensatory retribution, has never been far below the surface. Christians and Muslims share with Jews this deep flaw in human nature that so often affects our praying, both public and private. We may ask ourselves if there is an essential difference between the murderous 'heroine' Jael the wife of Heber the Kenite (Judges 5) and the murderous 'anti-heroine' Jezebel the wife of King Ahab (the villain of 1 Kings)? Or between Nehemiah the post-exilic governor of Jerusalem, and Ezra the post-exilic priest, both of whom are regarded as Jewish heroes and both of whom brought in to Jerusalem savage racialist laws aimed at establishing the same kind of 'pure race' that the Nazis were to practise on the Jews a long time afterwards, and the same separatist laws that successive governments of the State of Israel have practised on Palestinians? Nor were these essentially different from the Christian slave-traders of the eighteenth and nineteenth centuries in Britain, the Caribbean and America. We may also reflect that there is little to choose between medieval Christian crusaders and the Christian Phalangist warlords of Lebanon partly responsible for the slaughter of innocent Palestinian Muslim men, women and children in the refugee camps of Sabra and Chatila in Beirut[1].

In our contemporary society praying can never be the usually calm, comfort-seeking praying that perhaps most Christians seek; this is certainly so since Sabra and Chatila in Lebanon and since the slaughter by Christians of Muslims in Bosnia; and when, as Christians, we are tempted to point the finger at the children of Abraham who are not

By the rivers of Babylon we sat and wept aloud,
when we remembered Zion.
On the trees along the banks
we hung our lyres unused.
Our captors asked us there for a song —
those who had despoiled us, for music of joy:
Sing us one of the songs of Zion.
How should we sing the songs of the Lord
on the soil of a foreign land?
If I forget you, O Jerusalem,
may my right hand forget its powers.
May my tongue cleave to the roof of my mouth,
if I do not remember you,
If I do not exalt Jerusalem
above my highest joy.

Psalm 137:1–6
See Commentary by John Eaton[2]

Christians, we may before praying go back to our roots in the words of Jesus: **With the judgement you make you will be judged, and the measure you give will be the measure you get. Why do you see the speck in your neighbour's eye, but do not notice the log in your own eye?** (Matthew 7:1–5)

Iraq is certainly a very disturbing country to be in when it comes to praying with sense and sensitivity. As I travelled through Saddam Hussein's Iraq I reflected that the visionary prophet Ezekiel lived in exile in Babylon. The Muslim tradition is that he was buried not far from Karbela, one of the great Shia' holy cities of Islam whose people have been subjected to persecution and genocide by Saddam Hussein. There is a Jewish/Muslim shrine to Ezekiel, reminding us that the Old Testament prophets are honoured by Jews, Christians and Muslims alike. The experience of persecution and suffering should bring people together, and this surely is especially true of the children of Abraham. Islam describes Jews, Christians and Muslims as **ahl al kitab**, 'People of the Book', selectively identifying with varying degrees of interpretation the Old and New Testaments as holy scripture. At the same time our histories show a savagery that seems to be an accompaniment of religious fervour. The Jewish spirit of vengeance seen in many of the psalms and other parts of the Old Testament have been repeated so often in the actions of Saddam Hussein and his Ba'ath party officials, especially in the genocidal policies towards the Shiites, Kurds and the marsh Arabs of southern Iraq.

The uninformed use of language, even if it is not vocalised, is to be guarded against in prayer. We do perhaps take it too much for granted that public figures like politicians and news editors use language correctly. For example, many Christians, including myself, find ourselves labelled as 'anti-semitic' when in fact we are simply strongly opposed to the political Zionist State of Israel which has evolved from the central European atheistic dialectical materialism of Marxism in the nineteenth and early twentieth centuries; and our opposition is shared by the large number of Jews who are religiously Orthodox. In the same way the use of the word 'Islamist' has come to be used as a synonym for terrorism, and especially in Iraq and Afghanistan. However, the cruel and murderous policies of Iraq and Syria in the second half of the twentieth century and into the present century arise not from Muslim commitment to **sharia** law or Islamic constitutions, but from the secular socialism of Ba'athism in both countries (the name 'Ba'ath Party means 'The Renaissance Party'), It then does not take us long to realise that we Christians use the word 'Christian' to describe people who were simply born and brought up in societies having a history of Christian development, however secular they may be today: people who do not admit to having any religious or spiritual belief at all. This is a very unthinking use of language, given the violence of our modern world.

Because the Ba'athist regime in Iraq has been so vilified by Britain and the United States since the 1980s, when these nations stopped supplying arms to Iraq, my own travels through the country, together with visits to government ministers and officials, have made me reflect on the attitudes of influential Christians in their dealings with the Gulf States. There is much moralising in the statements of western politicians, especially perhaps those who possess a strong Christian faith; and in the statements of church leaders who seek to hold the high moral ground while supporting the prevailing political majority view. In our prayers we need to consider carefully whether double standards have any place in a life of faith. We practise double standards in the Middle East when we insist on obedience to United Nations' resolutions in some situations (usually those in which the western world has a vested political, military or economic interest) while ignoring their flagrant disregard in other situations; the contrast between western attitudes towards international law with regard to Israel/Palestine, Turkey and Cyprus on the one hand and Iraq, Zimbabwe and the Sudan on the other does not reflect well on political responses in the so-called Christian world. We applied double standards of the worst possible kind when Christian governments gave Saddam Hussein what he needed to wage war against Iran, but withdrew support when he worked against perceived western interests. We relinquish our claim as Christians to the high moral ground when we hunt down Saddam Hussein and his ministers but ignore the genocidal activity of President Mugabe and his ministers. The Christian world condemns countries like China, North Korea and Iran for building up nuclear stocks while its own most powerful representatives are the most prolific holders of nuclear weapons of mass destruction in the entire world.

The Church in Iraq [3]

A visitor to Jerusalem once asked the Palestinian wife of the then Anglican bishop in Jerusalem how long her family had been Christian. She answered, 'About 2000 years'.

In the very early days of Christendom, as the Acts of the Apostles shows, the main thrust of Christian evangelism was northwards from Jerusalem into Syria and westwards into Asia Minor (Turkey), Greece and Italy. We know, however, that it was not long, and probably even before all the companions of Jesus had died, that the Christian gospel

The Anglican Church compound and parsonage in Basrah after the Iran - Iraq War.

was proclaimed eastwards also, through Syria and into Mesopotamia (modern Iraq); then across the sea to India. Christian missionaries followed the incense and spice routes and, as we shall see later when we think about the more southerly parts of the Arabian Peninsula, the Christian presence was widespread in Arabia before the seventh century and the time of the prophet Muhammad.

In Iraq today there are Christians of a number of different Christian traditions, although the total Christian population is not more than one million, and since 2003 has been diminishing rapidly. When the Ba'athist Party ruled Iraq under Saddam Hussein, because of its secularist ideology, Christianity was openly practised without hindrance and the Christian traditions have always had high profile church buildings, including several cathedrals with patriarchs, archbishops, bishops and other church leaders. Since the western invasion of Iraq in 2003, with the consequent increasing communal disturbance between Sunni and Shia Muslims and the Kurds, the minority Christian groups are more vulnerable than they have ever been, especially as Islamic extremists, often from other Muslim countries, apply pressure for the establishment of an Islamic state.

Because of the extreme situation the condition of the Christian community in Iraq deteriorates all the time. Christians who have the financial resources are leaving the country in thousands and the most vulnerable, the poor, the elderly and children, are being forced out of the insurgency-controlled northern areas and seeking what shelter they can find in Baghdad. The great majority of the able-bodied Christian men have either been killed or have fled into neighbouring countries such as Syria and Jordan.

In Baghdad, the Anglican church of St George has a crucial role to play. After the first Gulf war of 1990–1991 the church was damaged and vandalised, but before 2003 it had been brought back into use. After the American and British invasion of 2003 the church suffered damage again but, now ringed round with security fencing and barbed wire, Iraqi Christians of different traditions, but scarcely any Anglicans, are maintaining their faith in God in Christ against all odds and a congregation of more than thirteen hundred people has grown up under the leadership and encouragement of the Anglican chaplain, Canon Andrew White.

St George's church is outside the protected international zone in Baghdad and Canon White wears body armour and moves around with security guards. The Anglican church has always stressed the importance of its vocation of hospitality and Canon White expresses this in the way he welcomes all Christians to St George's, without in any way attempting to proselytise. There is even a Mothers' Union branch of several hundred women and they devote much of their time to raising money to provide food and clothing for the many destitute people who enter St George's compound.

Inside the International zone Canon White and service chaplains lead worship at the Embassy for soldiers of all ranks and nationalities. Canon White is a Director of the charitable Foundation for Relief and Reconciliation in the Middle East, all of which needs prayerful thought and understanding.

There are many things in these last few paragraphs for us to reflect upon. As in Palestine/Israel, the real victims of the chaos and violence in Iraq are the poor, the children and the elderly, Christian and Muslim alike.

Christianity in Iraq, as elsewhere, has witnessed much division, especially in the early pre-Islamic centuries, and these divisions have severely limited the effective proclamation of the gospel; in the minds of Muslims the lack of Christian unity has reduced the credibility of the Christian insistence that it is a monotheistic religion. This is something for reflection, penitence and active prayer by Christians; also it is a challenge for Christians to try to understand what it means to be monotheistic with a Trinitarian belief in God.

Read Psalms 9 and 10

"(The Psalmist) shows a way of outspoken and passionate prayer against the cruel and on behalf of the helpless, a way that holds the evil up before God, and somehow holds on also to the all-encircling faith in the just Creator-King, the high tower for the poor, the one who raises his beloved from the gates of death. In Christian usage these psalms have brought to mind the strong prayers of Christ and his church for the poor and vulnerable, enfolding their sufferings in faith in the divine victory over cruelty and chaos. However great the troubles, the music of hope will ever sound before the Lord of the resurrection."

See John Eaton: The Psalms pp 82–86
Commentary on Psalms 9 and 10

The question of jihad (Holy War)
has been misunderstood.
It is essentially divided into two.

The Greater Jihad is fighting one's animal
tendencies. It is internal rather than external:
striving in the path of God to overcome one's
animal side. Man shares with animals certain
characteristics which, if let loose, make him a
very dangerous beast. To bring those passions
under control, that is what Jihad means.

Man has a tendency to overestimate himself
— and to underestimate his spiritual potential.
He has a tendency to control and exploit his
environment, and other human beings. Jihad is
essentially against such tendencies.
The Lesser Jihad — fighting on behalf of
the community, in its defence — is a duty
incumbent on a Muslim provided he is
attacked.
A man has the right to defend his life,
his property, and he has to organise himself
along these lines.

Professor Yusuf Ibish, quoted in
The Muslim Mind[4]

Let love be genuine;
hate what is evil, hold fast to what is good.
Love one another with mutual affection; outdo
one another in showing honour. Do not lag in
zeal, be ardent in spirit, serve the Lord. Rejoice
in hope, be patient in suffering,
persevere in prayer.
Contribute to the needs of the saints;
extend hospitality to strangers. Bless those who
persecute you; bless and do not curse them.
Rejoice with those who rejoice, weep with those
who weep. Live in harmony with one another,
do not be haughty, but associate with the lowly;
do not claim to be wiser than you are.
Do not repay anyone evil for evil, but take
thought for what is noble in the sight of all. If
it is possible, so far as it depends on you, live
peaceably with all.
Beloved, never avenge yourselves, but leave
room for the wrath of God; for it is written,
"Vengeance is mine, I will repay, says the
Lord". No, "If your enemies are hungry,
feed them; if they are thirsty, give them
something to drink; for by doing this you will
heap burning coals on their heads".
Do not be overcome by evil, but overcome
evil with good

Letter to the Romans, Ch 12, vv 9–21

Chapter 2
Kuwait
High tech. In the killing fields

Kuwait is Iraq's southern neighbour and it is a small desert kingdom compared with its more fertile neighbour and its more southerly neighbour the vast kingdom of Saudi Arabia.

The Al Sabah family has ruled Kuwait since the middle of the eighteenth century and has successfully made the transition from the simple Bedouin-style desert life to the responsibility for managing the development of the rich oil resources of the country and the modernisation programme carried out since the first export of oil immediately following the second world war.

Kuwait has always felt threatened by its immediate neighbours with their expansionist policies, but the Al Sabah family has maintained a beneficent paternalistic dictatorship which has ensured the channelling of oil revenues into the creation of a welfare society that benefits all indigenous Kuwaitis, especially in terms of health, housing, social welfare and education, from the earliest years and into the impressive facilities of the University of Kuwait.

What has always been lacking, as in most Islamic societies built on the dynasties of desert sheikhdoms, is the ability of citizens to express themselves freely and publicly in political matters. These societies are not naturally given to the principles of democracy as understood in western Europe and north America, and this has not been appreciated by western political leaders in the late twentieth and early twenty first centuries. It is partly this lack of understanding and appreciation that has led to the ill-conceived conflicts in the Arabian Peninsula and has led to a commitment, especially on the part of the United States, to impose western-style democracy upon societies which are singularly ill-equipped for it, unsuited to it, and whose mainline religion, Islam, tends to support alternative styles of government. The nations of the western hemisphere, with their Christian heritage, are prone to equate 'democracy' with liberal ideas and political freedoms as if they are of universal validity, while identifying undemocratic societies with tyranny, with terrorism, and as altogether needing to be changed; this demonstrates deep ignorance and arrogance and to make these contrasts is an entirely unacceptable and improper approach to people of cultures and religions other than ours. Christians need to ask themselves if forcing change on people by means of hi-tech warfare is the most enlightened way of living, and our answers to that question will affect not only the way we vote but also the way we pray. In any case, benevolent dictatorships such as Kuwait will, if left alone, evolve new and appropriate forms of government; their leaders are educated, intelligent politicians, educationalists and technocrats. Kuwaiti women are beginning to play, if not a dominant role (except in the family situation), at least a significant one, in the nation's affairs, and the royal family has begun to make serious headway in sharing government with a shura (consultative council); this follows an abortive attempt to form a National Assembly in the 1960s. Such moves as these will gradually introduce greater political freedoms into Kuwaiti society and it is a huge and costly mistake on the part of western democracies to suppose that they have the wisdom and the right to attempt to impose their own structures on Arab Muslim nations; this is amply demonstrated in the events in Iraq since 2003. All this is for Christians to reflect on as we watch television news and documentary programmes and read our newspapers.

Homelessness

When Kuwait was under Saddam Hussein's occupation between August 1990 and January 1991 most of the expatriates making up the work force fled the country, or were taken to Iraq as hostages. The majority were from the Indian sub-continent and the Philippines and many were Christian. There were also many expatriate Arabs, from Jordan, Lebanon, Syria and the North African countries; also many Palestinians who, because the Palestine Liberation Organisation openly supported Iraq in the conflict, were forcibly expelled after the liberation of Kuwait. The expatriate population in Kuwait just about exceeded the indigenous population and there was much suffering and deprivation in both communities. One of the worst examples of this was the fate of about four hundred and fifty Christian Iraqis who had lived and worked in Kuwait for more than twenty years. They were mostly affluent professional people: doctors, lawyers, engineers and such like, and they belonged to the Eastern rite Chaldean Catholic church, in communion with the Pope. After the liberation the Kuwait government decided not to renew their contracts and residence permits, simply because they were of Iraqi descent. They did not qualify for refugee status, so that they suddenly found themselves without work or any source of income, and homeless. The fate of these relatively few suddenly and totally deprived Christians kept me busy for some time, together with the Roman Catholic and Armenian bishops of Kuwait; in the end they were re-settled in Latin America. This seemingly insignificant spin-off from the Iraqi invasion of Kuwait is a reminder to Christians of all traditions that prayer for peace and justice needs to be validated by committed ecumenical effort to relief of suffering everywhere, whether few or many people are involved.

The question of refugees and other homeless people throughout the world raises large issues for Christians and challenges us to translate prayer into direct political action. The world responds quickly and generously whenever there are earthquakes and hurricanes and other natural disasters, but there is a tendency to hesitate when people are deprived of their human rights as a result of political activity. We have witnessed many examples of this since the end of the Second World War. The hesitation of the British government in dealing sympathetically with the Jewish exodus from Europe via Cyprus, the inactivity of Britain, Greece and Turkey over the 1974 invasion of Cyprus, when it was their direct treaty obligation to react, and the subsequent misery of thousands of Greek and Turkish Cypriots; the insensitivity of many nations in mishandling the Palestine refugee problem, or the callousness of previous victims — Jewish Israelis — in depriving non-terrorist and vulnerable Palestinians of their human rights by ignoring United Nations resolutions, culminating in the building of a high apartheid-

Then the king will say to those
at his right hand, "Come, you that are blessed
by my Father, inherit the kingdom prepared
for you from the foundation of the world;
for I was hungry and you gave me food,
I was thirsty and you gave me something
to drink, I was a stranger
and you welcomed me. I was naked
and you gave me clothing, I was sick
and you took care of me, I was in prison
and you visited me."
Then the righteous will answer him,
"Lord, when was it that we saw you hungry
and gave you food, or thirsty
and gave you something to drink?
And when was it that we saw you a stranger
and welcomed you, or naked and gave you
clothing? And when was it that we saw you sick
or in prison and visited you?"
And the king will answer them,
"Truly I tell you, just as you did it to one
of the least of these who are members of my
family, you did it to me."

Matthew 25:24–40

On her weak, shivering chest
hung a little thing as powerless
as a young bird.

She held his head with one arm
and embraced the body with the other.
She would have laid him in her bosom
had she been able to.

Perhaps by the warmth of her love
she would protect him against that freezing
night. He, while listening to her even
breathing, clasped his hands around her neck.

Then he muttered, "Mother",
his hands began fumbling at her neck and
cheek. Smelling in the baby the fragrance
of her usurped paradise, she heaped on him
fervent kisses.

From Ruqayya,
by Fadwa Tuqan, a Palestinian poetess[5]

style wall through the country and separating them from their means of livelihood. It was not a natural disaster that created the Lebanese civil war, resulting in the collusion of Lebanese Christians and Israeli Jews in the massacre of Palestinian refugees in the camps of Sabra and Chatila. These are simply examples that have affected my own life, but many more examples in other countries will occur to you as you reflect on the evil of selfish and cruel political and economic ambition and greed. We pray a great deal in our church worship services for a cessation of the appalling genocidal policies of the Sudanese government and insurgents alike towards the people of Darfur and others; when we begin to use our God-given brains and hearts in reflecting on many of these controversial events we may begin to understand that, far from being a bland, routine exercise of traditional pious duty, prayer might become alienating, leading to accusations of right or left-wing political bias, of anti-semitism and the like; when, in fact, none of these barbs are at all relevant to the real issue of our conversation with God, or to the absolute need for Christians to ensure that their prayers turn into the kind of social and political action that leads to the eradication of injustice, fear and destitution.

The killing fields

About twelve miles from Kuwait City and out into the Gulf south of Basra lies the island of Failika. One of the interesting characteristics of the relatively shallow water of the Arabian Gulf is that it holds fresh water springs; these provided a good source of water for human consumption from the earliest times and some of the small islands of the Gulf were inhabited. We know that people inhabited Failika from before 2000 BCE and Danish and French archaeologists in particular have excavated there for many years. The island must have been known to the traders and seafarers working between the Indian sub-continent and Mesopotamia and there are Babylonian texts that associate the settlements just off-shore from the Gulf mainland with the tales of Gilgamesh. Excavations have revealed signs of ancient worship, as well as a thriving trading post, with merchants' seals probably brought by sea to the Failika markets from the mainland. Three to four hundred years before Christ the island was settled by Greeks, who built a temple; by the fifth century CE there was a Christian community on Failika and the remains of a church have been unearthed. Two centuries later the Muslims would have arrived. All this on an obscure island in the Arabian Gulf, sustained by trade and acting as a stopover for seafarers on their way to distant lands.

Perhaps, then, we should not be too surprised that Saddam Hussein wanted to take possession of Failika for, instead of by-passing it in his invasion of Kuwait at the end of 1990, he invaded it and set up army camps on the island. There was of course no-one to fight, as the only people on Failika were fishing families, school teachers and archaeologists, and they were all sent to the mainland. When the allied coalition began to recover Kuwait in January 1991 they bombed Failika in a truly devastating fashion. In the soft sand of the island hundreds of cluster bombs from the allied aeroplanes failed to explode and their lethal contents were strewn all over the desert of Failika, mostly but not all protruding out of the sand.

Bomb disposal people, both military and private workers on contract, were eventually brought in to Failika to rid the island of these obscene weapons of mass destruction belonging to the coalition, and I was invited to spend a day with the teams. I learned the awfulness of these bombs and came to appreciate the courage of the men whose job it was to dispose of them. I was taught how to connect with electric wiring scores of them into squares and to find a wall to crouch behind and press the detonator; then to move on to the next square until many hundreds had been destroyed.

Throughout the day I found myself thinking about the children of Failika who were unable to return to their homes and school so long as these fearful bombs were on their island. Children who would, perhaps for years to come — on Failika and in unforeseen parts of the mainland — be kicking into the sand with their footballs and either killing themselves or losing limbs. All in the name of liberation.

The knowledge that this kind of thing goes on in many parts of the world, perpetrated by our own civilisation with its Christian history, confuses me when it comes to sorting out my prayers. Princess Diana and others have devoted much time and energy to the task of treating the destruction of unexploded mines and other lethal devices as a top priority, and in such circumstances this is probably the best kind of prayer.

Today there are happier developments in the saga of Kuwait. The new (2006) reforming ruler of the Emirate, Emir Sheikh Sabah al-Ahmad al-Sabah, is overseeing the development of Kuwait as a forward-looking nation, not relying entirely on the vast oil reserves (and the discovery of a new and huge natural gas field), but ploughing the immense wealth into welfare, technology of every kind, education, parliamentary reform which is leading to universal suffrage and the placing of women on an equal standing with men and, through a social development agency, ensuring that a great deal of the wealth of Kuwait is spread through the Middle East and Africa (non-Muslim nations as well as Muslim) for the alleviation of poverty. Those areas that were most distressed by the invasion from Iraq, including Failika island, are now being developed for tourism. Kuwait is beginning to show how the Muslim states of the Arabian Peninsula, none of which is naturally democratic, may develop a form of democracy within the paternalistic and benevolently autocratic Muslim systems. Under the new ruler, Kuwait has become an emirate where the powers of the ruling royal family are strictly limited and where even the ruler may be out-voted in the consultative council (Parliament); a society where women are beginning to take a lead in health and education and where they may have a voice in political decision-making. All this, connected with a tolerance and increased understanding of non-Muslim faith systems, could point the way forward to inter-faith dialogue, such as is happening in other parts of the Gulf; for example, Qatar (see below).

Our reflections and prayers are needed here, for Kuwait is still vulnerable to the passions of those who are committed to bringing about change through violent action. The Islamists of Kuwait are vocal in the consultative council and we need to understand that the potential power

Abandoning

I saw her
I saw her in the square
I saw her bleeding in the square
I saw her staggering in the square
I saw her being killed in the square
I saw her... I saw her...
And when he shouted
Who is her guardian?
I denied knowing her
I left her in the square
I left her bleeding in the square
I left her staggering in the square
I left her dying in the square
I left her...

*Samih al-Qasim,
Palestinian Druze poet[6]*

of their political voice is entirely due to the opening up of Kuwait by the royal family to some of the requirements of democracy. Learning that freedom brings responsibility, to self and to others, is difficult for Muslims, Christians and Jews alike.

Muslims restoring Christian parish life

Many Christian traditions are represented in Kuwait. The Anglican church building is in the oil town of Ahmadi, about thirty kilometres from the capital. Ahmadi is a thriving community of many nationalities and the headquarters of the Kuwait Oil Company (KOC) is there. Early

St Paul's Church, Ahmadi, Kuwait. Restored after the First Gulf War.

in 1991 I went to Kuwait to see what damage had been done to the church property. As I flew in to Kuwait International airport the dense black smoke of the still burning oil wells was rising from the desert around Kuwait and Ahmadi and we all knew that there was below us an ecological disaster on a massive scale. Apart from the native animals, such as the camels, sheep and goats, the thousands of migratory birds, such as cormorants, will be affected for a long time to come, and we have already thought about what has happened to the once-thriving fishing community on the island of Failika. There is also the massive pollution caused by the fleeing Iraqi soldiers, desperate to get home, and their pursuers. North of Kuwait City lies the Muttla Ridge, which since 1991 has witnessed to the folly of human greed and cruelty. The desert there is littered with the remains of burnt-out tanks and other military equipment, and there thousands of Iraqi soldiers died.

When I went back to Ahmadi I found St Paul's church and the clergy house badly damaged. The church needed re-roofing and re-decorating and the parsonage was totally uninhabitable. The ruler of Kuwait and the oil company had together given the land on which St Paul's is built, and had built the church itself, while the house was a gift from the authorities. I visited the General Manager of the KOC and he assured me that the church would be restored and another house found for the next clergyman, when I could appoint one. I visited HE Sheikh Sa'ad, the then Crown Prince and Prime Minister and he assured that he would personally see to it that the Christian community in Ahmadi and Kuwait was properly provided with everything it needed to worship freely and without anxiety; he reminded me that it is laid upon Muslims in the Quran and in the traditions to show every hospitality to non-Muslims living as guests in Muslim countries. The church in Ahmadi was restored and looked far better than before, while a good house was allocated for a priest.

On November 11th 1992 we had a service of remembrance in St Paul's and the dedication of a memorial plaque for the British troops who had died during the Gulf war. The Kuwait government showed its gratitude and generosity once more by inviting as guests of the government the next-of-kin and other relatives. The British commander, Sir Peter de la Billière, was present and read out the names. The families, most of whom had never been in a Middle Eastern country before, or met Arab Muslims, were given a full measure of Arab hospitality in a week of remembrance, of reflection and even celebration. These people, who had suffered great loss, were able to learn that Arab Muslims experience the same sorrows, similar regrets and the sense of desolation and abandonment that are shared by Christians.

**Waiting and watching
in sorrow and penitence.**

Out of the depths, Lord, I call to you;
O Lord, listen to my voice.
May your ears be attentive
to the sound of my supplications.
If you, Lord, retained offences,
who then, O Lord, could stand?
But with you there is forgiveness,
so that you may be feared.
I wait for the Lord, my soul is waiting,
and for his word I hope.
My soul looks for the Lord
more than watchmen for the morning,
yes, more than watchmen for the morning.
O Israel, wait for the Lord;
for with the Lord there is faithful love,
and with him is plenteous redemption,
and he will redeem Israel
from the bonds of all his sins.

Psalm 130

**In praise of the Creator and a
reminder of man's destructive power.**

You send the springs into the brooks,
to run among the hills.
They give drink to every creature of the field;
the wild asses quench their thirst.
By the brooks dwell the birds of the heavens,
and give voice among the branches.
From your high dwelling you water the hills,
and the earth is replenished through
all your work.
You make grass grow for the cattle,
and crops for the labour of the people,
to bring forth food from the earth,
and wine that gladdens their heart,
oil that makes their faces to shine,
and bread to sustain their heart.
The trees of the Lord are well nourished,
the cedars of Lebanon which he has planted,
where the birds make their nests,
while the stork has her house in the fir-trees.
The wild goats have the highest mountains;
the rock badgers find refuge in the cliffs.
How many are your works, O Lord,
and all of them done with wisdom!

Psalm 104:10–18, 24

There is no longer Jew or Greek,
there is no longer slave or free,
there is no longer male and female;
for all of you are one in Christ Jesus.
And if you belong to Christ,
then you are Abraham's offspring,
heirs according to the promise.

Galatians 3:28–29

Belief in one God brings us to believe in the
oneness of mankind. On the unity of mankind
is built the concept of human brotherhood.
This brotherhood includes all who believe
in God, whether Jews, Christians or Muslims.
These are "The People of the Book".
But this excludes those who are not believers
in God. This is a challenge to Islam, to broaden
its concept of human brotherhood to include
believers and non-believers.
Muslim mystics have been the forerunners
of such a broadening.
The famous mystic Ibn al-Arabi, for instance,
says that his brother is the other man,
regardless of his religion, race or colour.

Dr Hasan Saab[7]

Chapter 3
Bahrain
Oil wells and palm groves

In the northern western hemisphere a very substantial number of people from a Christian or nominally Christian background have a fear of the Islamic religion **(Islamophobia)**. This is often a silent repressed and suppressed fear, because the majority of western Europeans and Americans are probably naturally tolerant and generous people, as is frequently demonstrated when natural disasters occur in places where Christianity is not the faith of the majority. When terrorism strikes at the heart of society, as in the United States, Spain, Bali, Britain and other places, it is easy to point the finger at those professing a different faith and value-system from our own and judge the majority by the actions of a few.

Bahrain is a Muslim state that has demonstrated for many years that Christians and Muslims may openly practise their different faiths and at the same time live at peace with one another. Under the benevolent autocratic rule of the late Emir 'Isa bin Sulman al-Khalifa the Anglican cathedral of St Christopher prospered and acts as host to many small national Christian groups, especially the non-catholic groups from the Indian sub-continent. Similar tolerance has long been extended towards the Roman Catholic and Reformed Church in America congregations. Sheikh 'Isa died in 1999 and his tolerant and generous attitude towards the expatriate Christian population of Bahrain, most of them from the Indian sub-continent and the Philippines, has been continued by his son Sheikh Hamad.

Politically, Bahrain is placed in a difficult situation. It is an archipelago of more than thirty islands just over twenty kilometres out in the Gulf off the eastern coast of Saudi Arabia. The islands have been joined by causeways and the exploitation of the oil deposits since the 1930s has enabled Bahrain to develop into a modern state. The oil reserves

Islam and minorities: religious freedom.

As a religion, Islam does not put itself in an attitude of conflict towards other God-sent religions. The word Islam literally means surrender (to God). God's guidance has been sent through a succession of messengers and prophets who are all revered by a Muslim. Islam is thus the last link of a chain. The Quran reads:
"Say (O believers) we believe in God and in that which has been transmitted to us, and in that which has been transmitted to Abraham, Isma'il, Isaac, Jacob and the Tribes; and that which was given to Moses and Jesus; and that which was given to the prophets from their Lord. We do not discriminate between them and to Him do we surrender.

C Waddy[8]

will eventually run out and the government of Bahrain has developed a mixed economy with a strong emphasis on banking and investment corporations and the development of the port. The construction in the 1980s of the long causeway between Dhahran in Saudi Arabia and Bahrain causes tensions from time to time, especially as the liberal attitudes of the al-Khalifa family are not shared by the Saudis. In that part of the Gulf also the Shia' branch of Islam is in the majority and very strong in its expression: in the Eastern Province of Saudi Arabia, in Bahrain itself and not far east across the Gulf in revolutionary Iran.

Sunni and Shia'

The prophet and founder of the Islamic faith, Muhammad, died in 632 CE and immediately the matter of who should succeed him as **Imam** had to be resolved. Muhammad's successor, Abu Bakr, a member of the Quraysh tribe and a man related to Muhammad by marriage, succeeded in his assertion that Muhammad desired the succession to continue through the Quraysh and so it was that the Caliph 'Umar succeeded Abu Bakr. Not many years after the death of Muhammad and the first Caliph, the Patriarch of Jerusalem prepared to surrender the besieged city to 'Umar, who refused to receive the surrender inside the Church of the Holy Sepulchre. The treaty that was made contains the following: ('Umar) **grants to the people of Aelia** (Jerusalem) **security of their lives, their possessions, their churches, their crosses... they shall have freedom of religion and none shall be molested unless they rise up in a body. They shall pay a tax instead of military service... and those who leave the city shall be safeguarded until they reach their destination.** There was relative peace under the first two Caliphs but this was destroyed by political and religious disturbances under the third Caliph 'Uthman, who was eventually assassinated. The fourth Caliph, 'Ali, was a cousin of Muhammad and therefore the first blood relative to become Caliph; he was also husband to Fatima, Muhammad's daughter.

The term **sunna** refers to the Islamic tradition to which the majority of Muslims belong. This tradition adheres both to the teaching of the Quran and the customs and teachings of the first four Caliphs.

The election of 'Ali caused a good deal of dissension. Muslim armies had begun to march northwards and eastwards from Medina and their strong evangelical zeal brought them much success; however, it also produced rivalries and Muslims began to fight Muslims. Many of those who followed 'Ali were known as the **Kharijites**, which could be translated as 'the outsiders', because they began to interpret aspects of Islam rather differently from the majority party. One important aspect was that they believed that the voice of the whole Muslim community should be heard and heeded in decision-making, even for deciding on the succession to the Caliphate. The Kharijites were puritans, very strict and extreme in applying the law in matters considered to be offences against ritual purity. At length they broke away from Caliph 'Ali and others who honoured the traditions of the first four Caliphs. To the present day the Kharijites continue as a significant sect of Islam. 'Ali was murdered by the Kharijites in 661 CE and the **Shia'**, or **Shi'ites** ('sectarians' from shia', a party or sect) believe that Caliph 'Ali was the first Imam, because of his blood relationship with Muhammad; they were known as **Shia' 'Ali,** that is, the Party of Ali. However, the modern significance of the Shi'ites, especially in Iraq, Iran and other Gulf states where they have settled in significant numbers, lies in the story of Hussein, 'Ali's son and the Prophet Muhammad's grandson. Hussein had remained in Medina until, when the Ummayad Yazid was elected Caliph in Damascus in 680 CE, Hussein marched against him and was killed in battle at Karbala in modern Iraq. Hussein's body was savagely mis-treated, but eventually was buried in Karbala, which is now one of the great holy places and shrines of Shi'a Islam, together with nearby Najaf.

This brief diversion into some of the differences between *sunni* and *shia'* Islam is important for an understanding of the information that comes flooding into our minds through the newspapers, radio and television, and therefore affects our thoughts and the way we pray. It is important for us to realise that Islam has its problems of internal disunity and tension just as Christianity has, and that some Gulf states experience Muslim sectarian pressure just as Christians experience similar pressures in their practice of faith. In Islam, however, it is never a case of 'good' = 'traditionalist' = 'orthodox' Sunnis against 'terror-prone' = 'radical' = 'heretical' Shia'. There are many nuances to the titles sunni and shia' and both have a tendency from time to time to act towards one another with extreme violence, as we see in post-2003 Iraq. Stereotyping is unhelpful and misleading, while one of the worst examples of stereotyping is the uncritical, knee-jerk reaction of the power brokers in the United States towards Iran. In our conversation with God, insofar as we understand what we are doing, it is important not to project our own prejudices on him. A great deal has been going on in God's economy in places like Bahrain for many millennia, and to this we now return.

Bahrain has been known as a trading port for more than 5000 years, when it was part of the Sumerian lands. In the Christian period there were Nestorian settlements on this archipelago, with churches and monasteries existing under Persian rule. Bahrain became Muslim during the early years of the Muslim conquest and in the sixteenth and seventeenth centuries it was held successively by the Portuguese and the Persians. In 1783 the al-Khalifa family, who came to Bahrain via Kuwait and Qatar, took over the islands and have ruled Bahrain ever since. The British had some involvement in the management of Bahrain through treaties made with the al-Khalifa family between mid-nineteenth century and 1973.

This small group of islands has had a rich and varied history for thousands of years and has been influenced by very different religious traditions, many of which display a common interest in human origins, as in the stories of the Garden of Eden, the Fall and the Great Flood (the Gilgamesh Epic and the Book of Genesis, for example). Today, although Bahrain attracts tourists, it is not one of the booming tourist states in the Gulf, such as Dubai. In my frequent visits to Bahrain I was always able to reflect on the developing wonder of God's creation, that it was not a once-for-all event, but that it continues to evolve in wonderfully new and exciting ways; sooner rather than later the oil engineers will disappear from the region just as most of the pearl fishers have.

Bless the Lord, O my soul.
O Lord my God, you appear in glory.
You have put on majesty and splendour,
and wrapped yourself in light as in a garment.
You spread out the heavens like a curtain,
and in their waters laid the beams
of your high dwelling.
You make the clouds your chariot,
and ride on the wings of the wind.
You make the winds your messengers,
and fire and flame your servants.

May the glory of the Lord be for evermore,
and the Lord ever rejoice in his works,
who but looks on the earth and it trembles,
or touches the mountains and they smoke.
I will sing to the Lord as long as I live;
I will make music to my God
while I have my being.
So shall my song be sweet to him,
while I rejoice in the Lord.

Psalm 104:1–4, 31–34

Those in peril on the sea

Bahrain has always been important as a trading post for seafarers, and is so today. It also acts as base for American and British warships in the Arabian Gulf. In the conflicts at the end of the twentieth century and into the twenty first, between Iraq and Iran and through the invasion of Kuwait and the two Gulf wars, many ships, large and small, were struck by missiles and put into the port of Sitra, Bahrain, for repairs and the hospitalisation of members of their crews. Apart from the huge naval vessels, the smaller merchant ships are largely crewed by Filipinos and men from the Indian sub-continent. Many of them are not only at the mercy of the warring armies in the region; many ships are badly maintained and hardly seaworthy, and the crews are exploited by owners and agents. Port authorities quite often impound these vessels until they are made seaworthy and the bills are paid; in the meantime the crews are left high and dry, often not permitted to leave the dock area in ports like Bahrain for many months, and they remain unpaid and without the basic necessities of life.

This is where the work of the Anglican Mission to Seafarers and its Roman Catholic sister organisation is so important. Mission buildings with club facilities, libraries and, most important of all, international telephone links, have been built in many ports and are supported by willing and hard-working volunteers from the local churches, such as those in Bahrain. This work is a very good example of Christianity at work in what are sadly everyday situations in some of the Gulf states and many other parts of the world; it is prayer transformed into action.

The following is a piece for reflection, prayer and action taken from the Bahrain Anglican News, and was written by a chaplain of the Mission to Seafarers based in Bahrain; it describes a common situation among seafarers.

American Chaplains and the Provost of Bahrain with Bishop John during the first Gulf War.

A 100-foot tugboat with a crew of nine Filipino sailors engaged in supplying other vessels in the Gulf was detained in Bahrain's waters by a court injunction resulting from a financial dispute between the owners and the charter company. The crew were ordered to remain on board. During the following ten months one crew member died following a heart attack and four others have returned home. However, four crew members remain on board in deprived conditions anchored two kilometres off shore.

The Revd Victor Salve, chaplain of the Bahrain International Seafarers' Society (BISS), throughout this time assisted them in whatever way he could. His main concern was their repatriation and assistance with the supply of essential food and water.

Following the harvest festival weekend (in St Christopher's Cathedral) he made a visit to the tugboat in the company of Capt. Ali, the BISS Chairman and handed over some boxes of provisions. (The Chaplain writes) On behalf of the stranded seafarers I would like to sincerely thank the Dean, the members of the cathedral, the children of St Christopher's School and the Ecumenical Conference for the kind donation of provisions and food stuff as well as clothes to seafarers stranded off Bahrain. The generous donations were very much welcomed and gratefully received. Please pray that there will be a quick end to their suffering and that they go home as quickly as possible. Please hold them as well as their families in your prayers.

The Revd Victor Salve

Chapter 4
Qatar
Reality television

Qatar protrudes into the Arabian Peninsula like a thumb of the mighty fist of Saudi Arabia. The highest ground is 140 feet and the dry climate ranges from about 15–20 degrees Celsius in the winter to around 35 degrees in the summer months. It is a desert kingdom with a very modern capital city of Doha. The ruling family al-Thani are descended from bedouin Arabs; many members of the family have received higher education in the West and the urbanised inhabitants are occupied in technology and banking as well as in developing the largest gas field in the world. The majority of those living in Qatar are expatriates, chiefly from the Indian sub-continent and the Philippines, but with many also from the western and northern hemispheres as well as from other Arab countries. There are a great many Christian expatriates and the various church traditions are permitted to have public worship for their own adherents. Most of the Qatari Muslims belong to the Wahhabi sect of Islam. This is a puritanical branch of Sunni Islam and we shall be meeting it again when we are thinking about Saudi Arabia. However, the Qataris are not as strict as their neighbours, especially in their attitudes towards members of other faiths.

In connection with our prayers for the countries and people of the Gulf it is worth remembering that some of the nomadic people whose names are familiar to us in the Old Testament had settled in the Arabian Peninsula. In the case of Qatar, in the third millenium BCE Canaanite tribes were present, while in the first millenium BCE the political federation of Dilmun extended southwards from Kuwait and Bahrain, along the eastern regions of Saudi Arabia and into Qatar. There were certainly Christian settlements in Qatar in the early centuries of Christianity, as missionaries and Christian merchants of the Church of the East travelled southwards from what today is Iraq and established churches and monasteries at stopping places along the spice and incense routes.

In recent times most westerners have heard of Qatar because of the use by British and American television of Middle Eastern news coverage by the Qatar TV station al-Jazeera. This has brought a lot of unwelcome publicity concerning on the one hand the activities of western troops in Iraq, and the extreme cruelty of hostage-takers on the other. Television enables us to view instantly, and to assess instantly, the brutalising effects of war, and to see that civilised behaviour by one side in a conflict rather than the other can by no means be taken for granted. This is embarrassingly humiliating for democracies such as Britain and the United States, especially when the leaders of these nations are claiming the moral high ground in a conflict; and even more so when a significant number of those leaders are declaring their religious faith as an important basis for their political and military policies. When the President of the United States is reported as examining the option of destroying a news station such as al-Jazeera because of the adverse effects its broadcasts have on people's minds we need perhaps to be asking whether it is morally right (as distinct from politically expedient) for those of us who can claim some kind of Christian historical experience for our culture and democratic way of life to be dealing with terror by spreading our own brand of terror around the world.

I believe that this is where the message of Jesus Christ needs to be re-discovered by Christians, and this can be done only by careful exposure of mind and heart to his radical teaching concerning how his disciples should think and behave. Unfortunately, and distressingly for many Christians who wish to take their faith seriously, it is simply impractical to behave literally as Jesus of Nazareth would have us behave. It is difficult enough to face up to the realities of the (non-Christian) faith and practice of such as Mahatma Ghandi. If we take seriously Jesus' admonitions to go the extra mile, turn the other cheek, not to be judgemental, to bear the crosses laid upon us by our daily experiences in life, remembering the heroic way in which many of the Christians of the early centuries of persecution practised their faith, then we ourselves must seriously examine the way in which we respond to terror and its exposure by media. Our responses will have a direct bearing and influence on the way we pray, both verbally and meditatively.

In fact, far from approving terrorism through the media they control, the ruler of Qatar and his ministers are committed to a programme of inter-faith understanding and dialogue which attempts to take the emotional heat out of the political agendas of the western world and the Arab world alike. My own prayer about this is that such inter-religious dialogue will eventually begin to influence the mind-set of politicians in all the areas of conflict in the Middle East, as well as enabling reconciling conversation between Christian, Muslim and Jewish groups and individuals in North America and Europe.

When I say that this is my prayer it would be more accurate to say that it has been my prayer since 1954, when I took up a post as schoolmaster in St George's Anglican Cathedral school in Jerusalem. In all those years many good things have happened by way of Christian-Muslim understanding, but there is still so much to be done that intelligent prayer driving thought and action must not diminish for any reason, and especially because we may be tempted to think that nothing may be achieved and that the quickest way to achieve peace between communities of different faiths and cultures is to build ghettoes for each one. This is a lazy person's way to think and pray and act and the underlying argument is false; for example, the ugly tall separation fence being built in Israel to keep Jewish and Arab communities separate can only result in resentment, and not only on one side, and prevent the development of policies leading to reconciliation and peace-development. As I write there is news that the Saudi Arabian government is planning a separation wall along its border with Iraq. The idea is to prevent 'terrorists' or anti-Wahhabis (see below, chapter 8) from entering Saudi Arabia illegally, but it will only have the effect of isolating Saudi Arabia even further from its neighbouring Arab states than it already is. An even worse scenario would be the separation of the Sunni, Shi'ite and Kurdish communities in Iraq. It is also important to remember that there is in Iraq a very significant Christian community, dating from the earliest years of Christianity, which, because so many Christians are fleeing the country, is fast becoming non-viable.[9]

When we see these things happening we may wonder if we ever learned any lessons from the Berlin Wall, or whether, since 1967, Israeli Jews and Palestinian Arabs have learned any lessons from the days of the partition of Jerusalem or the isolation of the pre-1967 West Bank from the rest of the country.

So, while those of us who pray for peace in the Middle East and elsewhere between Christian and Muslim, may be tempted on occasion to cry out with the Psalmist, **O God, how long will you be absent from us, for ever?** we may in fact thank God for leading Muslim and Christian minds into fresh and sometimes exciting ways of meeting and

Worship in the English School in Dohar.
Plans for a new Anglican Church have been accepted.

learning how we may build bridges of reconciliation in and between our communities. The experience of Qatar is one to encourage us. When I first visited the Christian community in Qatar in 1987 I was expected to enter the country without showing any sign that I was a Christian priest or bishop, and my entry form was expected to state that I was a visitor to the British Embassy. The Roman Catholic Christians worshipped in an international school, and the Anglicans and other non-Roman Catholics were in an English school. Since then there has been a marked change in attitude, and now the Ruler has set aside land for church building. The Anglicans have ambitious plans to build a church and complex for inter-faith dialogue, with the resources for Christians and Muslims to learn about one another's beliefs and value-systems. These plans have the approval of the Ruler and already there have been meetings between senior representatives of the two faiths, including the Archbishop of Canterbury and Muslim leaders from al-Azhar University in Cairo. Much depends on the willingness, not only of Anglicans, but of the world-wide Christian and Muslim community, to contribute to the setting up of this irenic and ecumenical project which is designed to bring a new dimension to western and Arab thinking and behaviour in the Arabian Peninsula. Since the late 1970s most of us have been preoccupied with the military conflicts in the region: the Iran–Iraq war, the constant taking of hostages, Christian and Muslim alike; the genocidal activities of Saddam Hussein and the first and second Gulf wars. The concern of western nations has been to keep the oil flowing and the OPEC programmes under some kind of control. The concerns of the Palestinians and the powerful presence of Syria in the affairs of Lebanon have not been at the top of the agenda of Arabian Gulf states. Only in recent times, and in a totally spurious and uninformed way, has a religious dimension been introduced by the Saudi Arabian dissident Osama bin Laden and his supporters in Pakistan, Afghanistan, Britain and the United States; and, as we need to consider carefully, by the oil magnate and career politician George Bush and his supporters among leading British politicians. Few of these people, if any, show any real awareness of the roots out of which the monotheistic religions have sprung and the religious views expressed about unbelief, infidels, terrorism, inter-religious strife (for example, as between *Sunni* and *Shia'*), appear to be knee-jerk reactions based on whichever political, economic or social view the speaker happens to hold. The proposed worship and inter-faith dialogue centre in Qatar is designed to counter these aberrations and will attempt to bring together Christians, Muslims and, hopefully, Jews and others who are prepared to examine the validity and reality of living harmoniously as human beings within the paradox of diversity.

Elsewhere Christian-Muslim dialogue has been going on for a great number of years: St Cross College in Oxford, the Centre for Islamic Studies at Selly Oak (part of Birmingham University), the Royal Jordanian a:al al-Bayt Foundation under the sponsorship of HRH Prince Hassan of Jordan, the Centre for Jewish-Christian Studies, which includes dialogue with Muslims, at the Sacred Heart University in Hartford, Connecticut, the important work of the Missionaries of Africa (The White Fathers) reaching out from their Pontificio Istituto di Studi Arabi e d'Islamistica (PISAI) into the entire Middle East and those parts of Africa where Islam is a significant religion, and many other organisations in mainland Europe.

Part of the problem is the danger that all these well-intentioned organisations become intellectual hot-houses, with the Muslims tending to present legalistic prepared statements, and the Christians trying to decide whether to concentrate on social issues, such as the Family, 'Disappeared Children', the place of women in society, and so on; or to attempt some kind of dialogue concerning the doctrines that have evolved within the three monotheistic faiths and which have taken them a very long way from their common father Abraham. In my experience of attending many of these dialogue meetings real dialogue is rarely achieved and whenever there is a Jewish presence in the encounter, the political agenda of the State of Israel and the on-going preoccupation with the Holocaust tend to brush to one side the crucial attempt to work out in dialogue whether there is any real possibility that the three monotheistic faiths will ever, in their distinctive communities, be able to understand one another, appreciate one another's spiritual gifts, and live together in peaceful understanding that the one God of Abraham has made one world for all. I take up this subject in more detail in chapter 10.

The alternative, it seems to me, is that Jews and Arabs will go off into their spiritual deserts as Isaac and Ishmael took their separate ways, and that Christians will be left to decide whether they are really able to exist as children of Abraham and **ahl al-kita:b** ('People of the Book'), part of the monotheistic family with their distinctive Trinitarian doctrine of God as the father of the divine family of love.

There is no longer Jew or Greek,
there is no longer slave or free,
there is no longer male and female;
for all of you are one in Christ Jesus.
And if you belong to Christ,
then you are Abraham's offspring,
heirs according to the promise.

Galatians 3:28–29

[Christ] is our peace; in his flesh
he has made both groups
[i.e. Jews and Gentiles] into one
and has broken down the dividing wall,
that is, the hostility between us.

Ephesians 2:14

Allah is the light of the heavens and of the earth. His light is as if there were a lustrous niche, wherein is a lamp contained in a crystal globe, the globe as bright as a glittering star. The lamp is lit with the oil of a blessed tree, an olive, neither of the east nor of the west. The oil would well-nigh glow forth even though no fire were to touch it. Light upon light! Allah guides to His light whomsoever he wills. Allah sets forth all that is needful for mankind.

Al Quran: Sura Al-Nur 24:36ff
Trans. Muhammad Zafrulla Khan

In the beginning was the Word,
and the Word was with God,
and the Word was God.
He was in the beginning with God.
All things came into being through him,
and without him not one thing came into being.
What has come into being in him was life,
and the life was the light of all people.
The light shines in the darkness,
and the darkness did not overcome it.
There was a man sent from God,
whose name was John.
He came as a witness to testify to the light,
so that all might believe through him.
He himself was not the light,
but he came to testify to the light.
The true light, which enlightens everyone,
was coming into the world.

Gospel according to John 1:1–9

Chapter 5
The United Arab Emirates
Church planting

The United Arab Emirates (UAE) was formed in 1971 from the tiny desert sheikhdoms of Abu Dhabi, Dubai, Sharjah, Ajman, Umm al Quwain, Ras al Khaimeh and al Fujeirah. Some of these names and places are becoming very well known to Europeans, as the independent rulers in the Federation recognise increasingly that the vast oil fields will eventually give out and that, if the UAE states do not wish to revert to the relatively simple desert and maritime life of not so very long ago, other forms of revenue must be found and developed. Thus, **Abu Dhabi** is becoming a major sports and banking centre. **Dubai**, with its superb golfing facilities and its success in attracting major sporting events such as motor car racing, golf and world chess championships, has become a world leader in tourism. The smaller Emirates, reaching towards the Strait of Hormuz close to Iran, are trying to copy the example of the two big players. Abu Dhabi, Dubai and to some extent Sharjah, having been until comparatively recently small desert settlements with fishermen and pearl divers living around a simple fort, are now almost indistinguishable from Manhattan.

The rulers of the UAE are now, without exception, hospitable to their foreign non-Arab and non-Muslim work-force, who make up a large percentage of the population in each place. Abu Dhabi has a very high profile Roman Catholic cathedral, with a bishop and a large staff of priests and parish sisters serving the large Indian and Filipino populations. Christian worship is permitted, as in Bahrain and Kuwait, and on major Christian festivals many hundreds of Asian Christians and others spill out of the Roman Catholic cathedral and the multi-denominational Anglican church into the compounds. In a normal week it is expected that in these compounds, which have facilities for study, rest and refreshment, as well as for worship, there will be anything up to six or seven thousand Christians. In the context of what I am trying to do in these pages I am aware that this kind of information is astonishing and quite difficult to believe for many western Christians, who have been encouraged by the media to think of Muslim authorities in the Middle East in quite a different light. That is why I find it helpful to take each Muslim country on its own merits (and de-merits) rather than make sweeping generalisations that have no way of understanding the truth of a situation.

One of the more interesting small states in the UAE is **Sharjah**. It is true that there are high rise modern buildings, but the sheikhdom (which formerly housed a British Air Force base) is situated on a creek flowing out into the Gulf (as also is Dubai) where the building of sea-going Arab dhows goes on in a fascinating mixture of ancient skills and modern technology. Until the 1980s there was a maternity hospital deep in the old suq in Sharjah (the Sarah Hosman hospital) run by western missionaries, and numerous members of the ruling family were born there. The present ruler, Sheikh Dr Muhammad al-Qasimi, is a devout Muslim. He is also a scholar, having an earned doctorate of Exeter University. His generosity enabled the creation of the Exeter University Centre for Gulf Studies which provides many opportunities, not only for Arabic and Islamic studies, but also for Christians and Muslims to come together in dialogue and understanding. The Anglican diocese of Cyprus and the Gulf is also closely associated with the Anglican diocese of Exeter in a 'twinning' arrangement (together with the diocese of Thika in Kenya). In one way and another these and other links assist us in praying and thinking intelligently about the ways in which relationships between Christians and Muslims might develop peaceably without either Muslims or Christians compromising what is essential and fundamental to their beliefs.

A very interesting way in which we can see how wrong it is to stereotype people who do not share our beliefs concerns the tiny sheikhdom of **Ras al Khaimeh** (which means 'head of the tent' because of the way in which it protrudes into the Strait of Hormuz). When I first announced in the church in Dubai that I had an appointment to meet the ruler, Sheikh Saqr bin Muhammad al Qasimi, who is related to the Saudi Arabian dynasty, the Christians there became very nervous and promised me that they would be praying for me; it seemed that Sheikh Saqr had a fierce reputation, especally in his occasional and peremptory dealings with Christians. He permitted Christians in Ras al Khaimeh to worship privately and quietly in one another's houses and I was soon in the habit of celebrating the Eucharist in an apartment in a high rise block and even conducting Confirmation services in the upper room of an Indian takeaway!

On the day I first visited Sheikh Saqr I was met at his modest palace by his ministers and advisers, but chiefly by his western-educated sons. They were all robed in traditional Arab dress and greeted me with great courtesy. We waited in the **majlis** (the ruler's large meeting room — literally, 'the sitting place') and Sheikh Saqr arrived with his eldest son. I could see immediately that he was a bedouin both of the desert and the sea and he had the look of a fierce pirate. He sat me beside him and after the courtesies and the coffee drinking he began to ask me questions about the Christian church and how I found it in the Emirates and other places in the Muslim world. I was able to thank him for enabling Christians to practise their faith without harassment within his sheikhdom and to say how much Christians appreciated being able to attend worship in cathedrals and large church buildings in the chief cities like Dubai and Abu Dhabi. He immediately responded by speaking of the insistence of the Quran on tolerance and understanding between The People of the Book and spoke of the great responsibility Jews, Christians and Muslims have in maintaining the faith of Abraham. We spoke of the policies of Israel towards the Palestinians and the violent reactions of Hizbullah, Fatah, Islamic Jihad and the like. We spoke especially of Hizbullah and that led us on to Terry Waite and his fellow hostages in Lebanon. We discussed how religion could not and should not be assessed by its aberrations and in his view all religions have erred and needed reform. This led him on to the Protestant Reformation of the sixteenth century, about which he knew a great deal, and spoke of the Crusades as a crime, not only against Islam but also against the Orthodox of the East, and of the Inquisition as an aberration within Christianity. I was able to learn quickly that this simple and dignified sheikh, who was not in the least wealthy in the style of the rulers of Abu Dhabi and Dubai, and whose origins lay in the roaming life of the desert and in the traffic of dhows between the Gulf coastal ports and Iran; who spoke no English but who had made sure that his sons were highly educated, had an understanding of the origins and development of the three monotheistic faiths which enabled him to apply the fundamentals of these faiths to all that is going on in the world today. It is surely in ways like this, through the meeting of minds and devotional sense, that people of faith may come together and increase in mutual understanding and sympathy and make sense of their own conversations with God.

Church planting

It is important, when we are praying for the church in places like the Arabian Gulf, to remember that there are not many Anglican priests to each **country** we have been thinking about. In Europe now, especially in countries like Britain, we are accustomed to anything between a dozen and fifteen parishes being in the spiritual care of one full-time priest, with perhaps some assistance from non-stipendiaries, lay readers and retired clergy; in France it is now common for as many as thirty or more villages to be placed in the care of one full-time priest, with town parishes now often centering on one parish church.

When I first went to the United Arab Emirates there were four Anglican priests serving the entire area; one in Abu Dhabi, two in Dubai with Sharjah, and a chaplain of the Mission to Seafarers. The priest in Abu Dhabi had oversight of a large compound adjacent to an international school. The compound held a large Anglican church that was used also by Indian Christian congregations, and especially the Mar Thoma church. There was also a small and very beautiful Orthodox church. The chaplain then had responsibilities for an expatriate congregation in the university town of Al Ain, where the Anglican worship was held in the Roman Catholic church; he also went regularly to a house church in the westerly town of Ruweis and had an important ministry to the 'men-only' oil island of Das, about seventy miles out in the Gulf. The chaplain in Dubai had oversight of a large compound giving hospitality to many hundreds of mainly Indian Christians, in the large church and in the community buildings built around the compound. He had a full-time assistant in a church in Sharjah.

The scarcity of priests meant that each of them every week covered many hundreds of miles giving pastoral care to expatriate workers in the various Emirates: to Umm al Quwain (a house church), to Fujeirah, where there was a lively house church and where I baptised and confirmed in a hired room in a hotel; and to Ras al Khaimeh, which I mentioned above. There were also small, scattered communities of Christians in the Emirates: a community of Reformed church lay nursing sisters in Fujeirah, from Germany, Holland, Scotland and elsewhere and living simple lives in a small compound and caring for the poor of the town. There was a group of Indian Christians working on a chicken farm near Fujeirah and living in very basic conditions, as well as Pakistani Christians in a desert work camp, working on the public roads and gardens for long hours and little pay. When we went there I would celebrate the Eucharist on a simple table laid on the sandy floor with everyone sitting around cross-legged in the dust.

These were long journeys for the chaplain and always by road. These were long dual-carriageways across the desert and through mountains; and they were dangerous, as when darkness fell the camels, cattle and other animals tended to leave the desert and wander onto the roads where the tarmac warmed their feet.

Since the mid-1990s the patient work of the few chaplains in the Arabian Gulf from the 1950s onwards has been rewarded, and the quiet, peaceful way the many Christians go about their business in the Gulf states has been recognised by the rulers and senior government ministers, so that now in the Emirates there are five chaplaincy posts and two lay posts at the Resource Centre in Dubai; the work of the chaplain to seafarers has also expanded with the expansion of the port of Dubai and Jebel Ali. All this has been made possible, not only by the generosity of the Muslim authorities, but by the hard work of the lay people in the main church at Holy Trinity, Dubai. It has been made possible to worship in recognisable church centres in places like Ras al Khaimeh (St Luke's) and in the village adjacent to the growing port of Jebel Ali near Dubai (Christ Church), as well as in the well-established centres like Holy Trinity, Dubai and St Martin's, Sharjah. The importance of church planting is well understood in the Gulf, whether it is in the places already mentioned or in the Oman interior, the Yemen and Qatar. People sometimes ask me how Christians in the Arabian Peninsula deal with the prohibition on any attempt to convert Muslims to Christianity. My own thinking about this, in the years I have worked in Palestine, Jordan, the Sudan and the Gulf, has been guided by my understanding that it is God who converts any human being to himself, and that it is our vocation as human beings, whether we are Christian, Jewish, Muslim

Minibus of the Mission to Seafarers in Dubai.

or a member of any other faith, to grow nearer to him all the time in order that he may do his work in us. For Christians working in Muslim lands this is worked through by living faithfully as Christians, in the hope that our manner of life will enable God to work his good work in all the people with whom we have contact. This, of course, should be the pattern of Christian living everywhere, and it is certainly true in Europe that Muslims are deeply affected, as shown in their relationships with their children, by the increasing abandonment of Christian values by perhaps the majority of westerners. When a Muslim in, say, Bradford or Slough says, 'What is there in Christianity to command my attention?' what shall we begin to say?

Church planting happens when "two or three are gathered together" in Christ's name to pray, study, worship and serve. The calling to do these things combines both faith and works and in their faithful application God's law is fulfilled. Muslims understand this kind of language when they see it happening in the lives of Christians; those in the Arabian Peninsula are showing this witness in their lives, often in very challenging situations.

I planted, Apollos watered,
but God gave the growth. So neither the one
who plants nor the one who waters is anything,
but only God who gives the growth.
The one who plants and the one who waters
have a common purpose, and each will receive
wages according to the labour of each.
For we are God's servants, working together;
you are God's field, God's building.

1 Corinthians 3:6-9

The Lord appointed seventy others
and sent them on ahead of him in pairs to
every town and place where he
himself intended to go.
He said to them, 'The harvest is plentiful,
but the labourers are few; therefore ask
the Lord of the harvest to send out labourers
into his harvest'.

Luke 10:1–2

**Say, The kingdom of God
has come near to you.**

Luke 10:9

**[Allah speaks]
Assuredly, We have created man and we know
well what kind of doubt his mind throws up.
We are closer to him than his jugular vein.**

al-Quran 50:17

**The righteous shall flourish like a palm tree,
and grow like a cedar in Lebanon.
They are planted in the house of the Lord;
they flourish in the courts of our God.**

Psalm 92:12–13

Chapter 6
The Sultanate of Oman
The generous land

High mountains and desert with a long, almost deserted coastline make Oman one of the most naturally beautiful countries in the Middle East. It is a fascinating mixture of old and new. Muscat is the capital which, together with its suburbs, today stretches many miles. Muscat itself has a 'toy-town' aspect to it, especially around the palace and modern government buildings, with ultra-modern hotels and residential areas. At the same time there is a well-preserved fish market and ancient suq around the harbour. Most Omanis wear traditional long-flowing robes, distinctive head-dress and the Omani curved dagger signifying adulthood, worn proudly, and happily, for decoration. Together with its neighbour, The Yemen, Oman has retained its Arab characteristics, especially in the interior where the old forts and water channels (Arabic **falaj**, pl. **afla:j**) are much visited in a country which is increasingly opening up to tourism.

The approach to Muscat from the sea is dominated by two Portuguese forts guarding the entrance to the harbour. These date from the Portuguese occupation between 1507 and 1650. The Dutch and Iranians had interests in Oman and treaties were made with Britain through most of the twentieth century.

The present ruler, H.E. Sultan Qaboos ibn Said, is tolerant and generous in his dealings with the very large Christian expatriate population; as with the other countries we have been thinking about these are from every quarter of the world, but especially from the Indian sub-continent and the Philippines. The ruler is a very interesting person. He was educated for a time at a private preparatory school in an East Anglian Vicarage, run by the Vicar and his wife. This gave Sultan Qaboos a life-long interest in organ music and a liking for Anglican chants; he is a well-known musicologist and encourages the musical education of

The fish market in Muscat.

Omani children. The Sultan is also a graduate of Sandhurst Military Academy and the military band of the Omani armed forces is excellent. In recent years a new church has been built in Sohar in the north of the country; we know that there was a Bishop of Sohar in the fifth century and it is a cause of great thanksgiving that a Muslim ruler has restored the Christian presence there.

A Middle East saint

I have taken the following piece from a booklet by Bishop Kenneth Cragg about holy men and women who have served the church in the Middle East. Just outside of Muscat there is a cove known as 'cemetery cove'. It is a quiet spot for meditation and reflection and contains the graves of diplomats, sailors and missionaries (especially those of the Reformed Church in America) who have served God in Muscat and Oman with great faithfulness. One of these graves is that of Thomas Valpy French, an Anglican bishop of whom Bishop Cragg writes:

Muscat claimed Thomas French for only four months after a long ministry from 1851 to 1888 in India. Born in 1825, the son of a vicarage, he had a brilliant career at Oxford before volunteering for teaching in India. He helped in the foundation of St John's College, Agra (the city of the Taj Mahal), which became one of the greatest Christian institutions in Indian education.

Thomas French was also a keen evangelist and spent some time on the borders of Afghanistan before ill-health compelled him to withdraw. Physical frailty dogged him for many years but did not prevent him from a whole decade of vigorous leadership, from 1878 to 1888, as the first bishop of the vast diocese of Lahore. There he built the splendid Cathedral in the Mall and left a living legacy of pastoral vision and saintly example.

Ten years of Diocese building had not wearied his ardent spirit. Though the Church Missionary Society could not support him in the venture, he volunteered, at sixty-six, for evangelism in Muscat. It was there that he died and his grave lies in a sandy cove, reached only by boat, under the dark, basalt cliffs of the Omani coast.

Invited on arrival to have his quarters in the
British consulate, he declined, though it was
his best, perhaps his only, hope of escaping
disease and squalor. He did not wish
his mission for Christ to be identified, however
strongly, with British 'interest'.
His decision cost him his life. The world might
say that in his state of health it was a
foolish gesture. Not so, the love of Christ.
The spur of it brought young Americans,
Zwemer and Cantine, to begin the
Arabian Mission in the Gulf.

Prayer

With the holy and humble of heart,
we bless the Lord, rejoicing in their fellowship:
among them your servant Thomas French,
teacher, bishop, evangelist,
shepherd and seeker of souls.
Renew in your Church today the same
loving zeal and grace, through the indwelling
of Christ as Lord.

Bishop Kenneth Cragg[10]

Listening with concentration: a cautionary tale

During the many times I have sat with Muslims speaking of those things having to do with God and faith, I have come to understand the absolute need to concentrate with the whole of one's attention on what is being said. It is one thing to hear the sound of words; it is quite another to listen attentively. The danger of misunderstanding is particularly acute when carrying on a conversation in a language other than one's own, but it is something about which care has to be taken at all times, including leading prayer in church or a prayer group, and listening to other people praying. I am bound to say that I have heard a good deal of nonsense being spoken during intercessory prayer over many years, and I have no doubt that I have myself slipped up from time to time.

I once visited the Grand Mufti of Oman with the local chaplain. The Mufti brought along a number of students from his **madrasa** (religious school) and a translator to help the chaplain who could not speak Arabic. The Grand Mufti was keen to examine me on theological issues that particularly concerned the leaders of the sixteenth century Reformation, like Martin Luther. We spoke about our understanding of salvation by faith through grace and about the person and teaching of Jesus (called **Isa** by Muslims). The Grand Mufti was well educated in Christian theology and he showed a detailed knowledge of the teachings of Martin Luther. As we spoke I tried to listen carefully to what the Mufti was saying to me in Arabic, and on my other side I could just make out what the translator was saying to the chaplain. I suddenly realised that the translator was speaking all the time about Martin Luther **King**! Because of a long story in that morning's Omani newspaper about the American Baptist preacher the entire conversation between the Grand Mufti and myself had been totally misunderstood, for the translator's thoughts were elsewhere. That day I learned an important lesson about attentiveness and concentration.

Ibadhism

During the seventh century CE, the new faith of Islam spread rapidly throughout the Middle East, converting mainly polytheistic communities, but also some that were Jewish and Christian. Sometimes the conquest was military, sometimes peaceful, and often a mixture of the two. As the armies moved about it was inevitable that their leaders would impose their own interpretations of Islam upon the newly converted communities. Early on the city of Basra at the northern end of the Arabian Peninsula became an important centre for the new faith and its armies. Although the word **Ibadhi** refers to a certain Abdullah Ibadh, the Ibadhis follow the teachings of a scholarly Omani from Nizwa in the Oman interior named Abu Shaath Jabir ibn Zaid. He influenced people in Basra and was highly respected as being close to those who had been in the Prophet Muhammad's inner circle.

In early Christianity, as we know from the Acts of the Apostles, disagreements over interpretation of Jesus' original teaching soon appeared. The same thing happened in the early development of Islam and by the last quarter of the first Muslim century (approximately 675 CE onwards) there were religious leaders who were anxious to return to their founder's fundamental teachings and restore the original purity and essential simplicity of the faith. The Ibadhis struggled to re-establish this simplicity and specifically rejected the idea of dynastic rule in Islam through the Prophet's family, preferring to have a leader in the faith who would be acceptable to the **'umma** (that is, the entire Muslim nation) for his learning, piety and devotion. This movement spread from Basra into Persia and India and southwards back into Oman and the Yemen Hadhramaut. It moved also into North and East Africa and eventually into Spain.

The Ibadhis of Oman, while very orthodox and applying sharia law, have generally shown a tolerant spirit towards those who disagree with them, and no more so than today. Worship in the Ibadhi tradition is quiet and simple. Only in recent years have the city mosques become extremely large and ornate, with much gold leaf decoration. In the villages, however, the small community mosques appeal in their simplicity and glistening whiteness, reflecting the quiet dignity of the people that is so characteristic of the Omani people today.

In the western and northern hemisphere we have become accustomed to demonising Muslims and it is therefore important to learn not to generalise. The majority of 'ordinary' Omanis, like so many 'ordinary' Christians, are people trying to make sense of their lives in a bewildering, changing world. Just as there is growing evidence in Christian communities that many people have some kind of belief in 'spiritual' matters (a power, or powers, beyond our own natural powers), but increasingly finding the institutional churches lacking in credibility, so also, given the necessary changes in demographic, social, economic and faith make-up, do Muslims. The churches exhibit deep divisions within and between themselves, and Muslim communities do the same, as we witness between Sunni and Shia communities in Iraq and other countries of the Arabian Peninsula. All this argues for an understanding dialogue through prayer and reflection, with God and with each other, within and between the various faith communities, monotheistic and otherwise. But this must not be carried on simply at the levels of leadership and scholarship; it must begin and be developed in our small, local praying and worshipping communities.

Biblical Imperatives:

Be of the same mind;
have the same love;
be in full accord;
be of one mind.

Philippians 2:2

In the Arabian Peninsula Christian unity is an imperative that must be exhibited openly in the **will** of all Christians, in the **prayers** of Christians and in the actual **accomplishment** of Christians. Anything less is to give, in the spiritual centre of the Muslim world, a completely false picture of what Christianity is really about. Oman is a good place to consider this and the un-Christ-like nature of Christian disunity, but it is of universal application.

I have already spoken of the generosity of Muslim rulers, such as Sultan Qaboos of Oman, in giving land for the use of Christians and the building of churches and facilities for multi-denominational worship and meetings. The usual practice throughout the Gulf in places where this is permitted is for the Catholics (Latin and Eastern rite), Orthodox communities, Anglicans and the Reformed Church in America to be given land in the expectation that they will provide adequate facilities for other Christian groups. In this way the compounds of the mainline churches are filled by many hundreds and sometimes thousands of Christians through the week. They are members of Pentecostal churches, New Life congregations and many others that are sprouting up almost every month. Those who in their home countries would attend Presbyterian, Methodist or Lutheran churches, for example, tend to worship with the Anglicans or Reformed Church.

The real problem is that, as Christians, we are reluctant to admit that many of these new groups come about because of the quarrelling and dissension in the parent group; power struggles are common within churches and people, often totally unqualified, apart from their intense zeal for the gospel, lead breakaway groups and establish new congregations in hired rooms or in one another's houses. When this happens it is not long before new bureaucratic rules are in place, often tending towards rigid autocracy, and new dogmas arise resulting from ill-considered private interpretation of scripture.

If all this seems harsh, I think our consciences will tell us that it is a process happening all the time in churches throughout the world. In developed urban societies in the western and northern hemispheres, as well as in Australasia, the proliferation of new church groups is very common, usually taking the form of breakaways from the mainstream churches and, because society is becoming increasingly secular, no-one cares very much. But where it happens in countries where Christians are a small minority, as throughout the Arabian Peninsula, then Christian quarrelling and dissension leads to disunity that is scandalous in the biblical sense of being a **cause of offence and a stone of stumbling**, and deeply sinful.

There is much need for all of us to recognise, deep within our meditation and our prayer, that by our disunity we not only impair our relationship with one another, but we impair also our relationship with God. In the Arabian Gulf states, while Christians tend to call themselves 'Christian' rather than 'Anglican', 'Catholic', 'Reformed', and so on, the differences between and within Christian communities are often so marked, leading to judgmental attitudes, that if any Muslim should be inclined to turn to Christ as Lord and Saviour it would be very confusing for him or her to decide which Christ to choose. These examples of what may happen in areas where there are only small numbers of committed,

A service of dedication at the new Church of the Good Shepherd at Ghala in the capital area of Muscat. This church was badly flooded in 2007.

practising Christians may remind those of us who are Anglicans how deeply sinful are the divisions between large groups of Christians who should, under God, **be of the same mind** and **have the same love** as is seen within the divine family of Father, Son and Holy Spirit; and especially between African dioceses where there are vast Muslim populations, as in Nigeria, and American dioceses which need to be vigilant for the gospel in a country that follows a free market agenda, not only in economics but in religious matters also.

None of this is new, but it is not often sharply addressed and, as I hope we are seeing, our conversation with God needs to be sharply focused on the truth about ourselves actively searching out his will rather than telling him about our own virtues. In a divided and violent world with monotheistic and monolithic Islam in the ascendancy, the unity of all Christian people is crucial: unity between our separated churches but also within our own church communities and congregations.

Now I appeal to you, brothers and sisters,
by the name of our Lord Jesus Christ,
that all of you should be in agreement
and that there should be no divisions
among you, but that you should be united in
the same mind and the same purpose.
For it has been reported to me by Chloe's
people that there are quarrels among you,
my brothers and sisters.
What I mean is that each of you says,
'I belong to Paul', or 'I belong to Apollos',
or 'I belong to Cephas', or 'I belong to Christ.'
Has Christ been divided?
Was Paul crucified for you?
Or were you baptized in the name of Paul?

1 Corinthians 1:10–13

Let the same mind be in you that was
in Christ Jesus, who, though he was in the form
of God, did not regard equality with God as
something to be exploited,
but emptied himself, taking the form of a slave,
being born in human likeness.
And being found in human form, he humbled
himself and became obedient to the point
of death — even death on a cross.

Philippians 2:5–8

**At the name of Jesus
every knee should bend,
in heaven and on earth and under the earth,
and every tongue confess
that Jesus Christ is Lord,
to the glory of God the Father.**

Philippians 2:10–11

Chapter 7
The Yemen
Arabia Felix?

The Yemen might easily be regarded as the most beautiful and dramatic country in the Middle East. From Aden on the southern coast and the western desert plains bordering the southern part of the Red Sea the land rises from sea level through fertile terraced mountains reaching over 12000 feet to the capital Sana'a. In ancient times the Yemen was part of the region called "Arabia Felix" — 'Happy Arabia' — and around the time of Solomon it was called Saba after the ruling Sabaeans. This is traditionally associated with the biblical Sheba and its queen (see 1 Kings, chapters 2–1 for the story of Solomon, and chapter 10 for the visit of the Queen of Sheba). This story tells of the great importance of the spice, incense and gold routes from the Gulf of Aden in the Indian Ocean and northwards to the great trading centres of Alexandria, Jerusalem, Damascus, Baghdad and Basra en route to Persia and the Far East.

In modern times many people have been entranced by the Yemen. Freya Stark wrote eloquently of the Hadhramaut and Wilfrid Thesiger travelled the Empty Quarter through the Yemen, Saudi Arabia, Oman and through to the Emirates. In our own time the traveller and writer Tim Mackintosh-Smith has made Sana'a his adoptive home and brought to life the wonderfully rich culture and human characteristics of this land.

By the fourth century CE Christian missionaries had travelled to the Yemen and there was a huge Abyssinian cathedral in Sana'a, where there is now a large mosque. Christian travellers, probably sea merchants, were known to have been on the island of Suqutra, between the Yemen and Somalia, well before the Muslim conquest; the sixth century monk Cosmo Indicopleustes, says that the islanders were Nestorian Christians[11]. With the Muslim conquest in the seventh century the Yemen was ruled first from Damascus and later from Baghdad. The Ottomans ruled for many centuries until World War I, when northern Yemen became independent.

Sana'a Old City, Yemen.

The British controlled Aden from 1839 until 1967 when southern Yemen became a Marxist Republic.

The story of the Yemen in modern times has been the familiar one of power struggles between feudal monarchs struggling to hold on to power against the territorial ambitions of warlords and the ascendancy of modern political ideology, such as Soviet Marxism.

In the end and after many years of negotiations between the Islamic northern Yemen and the Marxist south, the two parts of the country were unified in the early 1990s. Good relations between the Yemen and its Arab neighbours have always required high levels of diplomatic skills, as medieval Yemen in the twenty first century struggles to come to terms with the modern Middle East. Tourism begins to be encouraged in this lovely land, but the Yemen supported Saddam Hussein in the first Gulf War of 1990–1991, which did not endear it to Saudi Arabia and the Gulf States. America and Britain regard the country as a training ground for international terrorism, which is the kind of unthinking generalisation this book is wishing to eradicate.

In all this turmoil and occasional unrest, the Christian church is tolerated and actively encouraged by officialdom if it can be seen to be socially concerned and beneficial to a country that ranks as one of the world's poorest. The church responds to this need in a number of important ways.

The Sisters of the Poor

For many years the Sisters belonging to the community of the late Mother Teresa have worked in the Yemen. These Sisters are chiefly from the Indian sub-continent and have four areas of work in the country. In Sana'a there is a home for very severely disabled children, the majority of whom have severe motor disabilities and are unable to walk or even stand. Their families are unable to cope and the Sisters pour out love and devotion on these children. They are helped by volunteer members of the Sana'a expatriate community, Roman Catholic and other Christians, as well as concerned humanists. These people, of faith and no faith, whose lives are very different and affluent, wash the children and play with them as far as that is possible; they are able to witness to the miracle of distressed children's faces lighting up and breaking into smiles, and they send out a silent message of how wrong it would be to allow these children to die at the point of birth or earlier. My own life has been much changed by the poor, the helpless and the outcast: by Arab refugees in the post-1948 camps of Jericho and Bethlehem, by leprosy sufferers in the mission hospital of Omdurman, Sudan, and by a severely disabled young Muslim Yemeni girl in the care of the Mother Teresa Sisters in Sana'a, who eventually began to recognise me on my occasional visits and looked to me to pick her up off the floor, hold her like a rag doll and slowly gyrate around the simple ward with her to the dance music blaring from her transistor. Not only her face, but her entire

*The Leprosy Hospital in Ta'iz, Yemen,
run by The Sisters of the Poor (Mother Theresa's Sisters).*

broken body became a smile. As I look back I understand that this too is a way of prayer.

In the Red Sea town of Hodeidah the Sisters have a home for the elderly severely disabled and those suffering from various forms of dementia. Again, these Yemeni Muslims have been rejected by their families, often left at the Sisters' gate, and come to know the commitment to the poor and outcast and the love dispensed by the Sisters. In the former capital of the Yemen, the mountain city of Ta'iz, and in Aden, are two more homes run by the Sisters of the Poor. One of them is for leprosy sufferers, outcasts from their own families and communities who know full well what it is like to live in darkness. This compound for lepers is called **'madi:nat an-noor'**, that is, 'City of light', which explains it exactly. All of these compounds make a major contribution to the quality of life of many Yemenis, young and old, who otherwise would have none at all.

Also in different parts of the Yemen are hospitals, clinics and schools run by other non-Roman Catholic church agencies, as well as there being a strong United Nations refugee relief service in the country. There is a long-standing Baptist hospital in Sa'ada in the remote north of the country, and another Protestant hospital at 'Ibb in a mountain valley near Ta'iz. Life is simple and basic and sometimes dangerous for the missionaries and it is not many years since some of the medical missionaries at 'Ibb were murdered by a deranged Muslim extremist. Whenever this kind of thing happens there is a loud outcry or shocked anger from the government and ordinary members of the public. It is a sad way for a sick individual to seek public acclaim.

A Grand Mufti's fatwa.

Many westerners are now familiar with the Arabic word **fatwa**, because of the fatwa that was delivered on the writer Salman Rushdie after the publication of *The Satanic Verses*. The word means **'a formal legal opinion'** relating to the Muslim religion and it may be delivered by a Muslim religious leader qualified to deliver legal opinions. These

Christ Church, Aden.

*Top and middle:
Before restoration.*

*Bottom:
Christ Church restored.*

opinions are delivered not only against someone or something, as in Rushdie's case, but they may also be delivered in support of a person or project, as in the story I am about to relate.

In the late 1980s when southern Yemen was still a Marxist state, I was very keen to restore one of the Christian churches in Aden that had been used by the British military until 1967; in the intervening years these had become storehouses and sports halls and one of them had become an interrogation centre for the dreaded Marxist security police. I found the authorities very cooperative and by the time Marxism collapsed and the south and north of the Yemen were well on the way to unification I had settled on a plan to restore Christ Church, Steamer Point, Aden, in the district called Tawa:hi, which was close to the harbour and used by the Yemeni navy. The plan included the creation of a medical clinic for local mothers and their small children. I began fresh negotiations with the new government of the united Republic of the Yemen in Sana'a and at the same time formed a friendship with the Grand Mufti of the Yemen, HE Grand Mufti Zabarah, who lived in one of the wonderful tower houses in the old city of Sana'a. The Grand Mufti was very supportive of the plan and in due course he delivered to me a fatwa, which translates as follows:

In the name of Allah

I hereby issue my formal religious rule stating that there is no objection for the church in the city of Tawahi, Aden, to continue conducting religious services, and to allow it to be renovated. It is our duty to allow members of the Christian community to exercise their religious rites, and to worship in their churches, as it is the case in our mosques and Islamic centres all over the United Kingdom and the rest of the Christian world.

(signed) Grand Mufti Zabarah of the Yemen

The Clinic.

The queue starts early in the morning.

The Mother and Baby Clinic in Christ Church, Aden, Yemen.

This underlines much of what I have tried to say here about the importance of not generalising about religious faith and practice; in this case, Islam. In many ways the Yemen is still a medieval country, with modernism struggling with feudalism, and both struggling with Islamic fundamentalism. At times violence breaks out and it is dangerous to travel around. At the same time most of the people are extremely hospitable and friendly, in the manner of the majority of Arab people throughout the Middle East. As a result of the fatwa we were able to restore Christ Church and start work on a clinic in the compound. Isolated attempts to interrupt and even destroy the project have been thwarted by Adeni mothers with their young children queueing every morning to receive medical help. Medical volunteers have been found from various European countries and the Commonwealth and supplies of drugs and other medical equipment were freely sent by well-wishers. My successor continued and developed the work and a chaplain is in post. Christians in many parts of the world have recognised the importance of turning prayer into action when it comes to healing desperately poor people in one of the most deprived countries of the world. The Aden clinic has now developed outreach work into the outlying villages and works closely with the Sisters of the Poor and much-needed eye treatment is being developed. Relying on volunteers is never easy, but it is important that this work does not lose its impetus.

The strength of prayer and solidarity of the Christian community.

There is much going on in the Yemen by way of Christian work and commitment. In such a vast country, where the larger centres of population are cut off from one another by deserts and ranges of high mountains, it is not always easy to identify what the Christian church is up to. Christians living in the Yemen of whatever nationality and whatever church tradition tend to call themselves 'Christian' rather than apply denominational labels to themselves and in this way the witness of all Christians becomes unified as the witness of a single community of faith and a common commitment to a single fellowship in the faith of Christ.

Ointment and Dew for a Needy World

See, how good and how pleasant it is,
when pilgrims dwell together as one.
It is like the precious ointment on the head,
that ran down upon the beard,
ran down upon the beard of Aaron,
and on the collar of his garments,
as though the dew of Hermon
ran down on the hills of Zion.
For there the Lord
has commanded the blessing,
even life for evermore.

Psalm 133

Prayer

Grant to your people,
good Lord, the spirit of unity, that they may
dwell together in your love, and so bear to all
the world the ointment of your healing
and the dew of your blessing.[12]

Chapter 8
The Kingdom of Saudi Arabia
The unyielding land

When we begin to reflect on the religious, political and economic situation in this final country of the Arabian Peninsula, we shall quickly see why it is necessary never to generalise about Muslim Arab countries in any way. I was once in a meeting in London with the Saudi Arabian ambassador to the United Kingdom, trying to reach an understanding about my role as bishop in Arabia at a very difficult and sensitive time. At one point the ambassador said to me, 'Understand, bishop, that the Kingdom of Saudi Arabia will never behave towards non-Muslims in the same way as the other liberal Arab states in the Gulf.'

The vast country of Saudi Arabia is made up of mountains and desert with ultra-modern cities on the western coast bordering the Red Sea (al-Hija:z) and on the eastern coast bordering the Arabian Gulf (ash-sharqiyya). Inland are the Muslim holy cities of Mecca and Medina and the capital city of Riyadh.

In the early part of the sixth century CE the entire area was made up of tribal communities, chiefly polytheistic but with considerable settlements of Jews and Christians. Nestorian missionaries from the north, together with Monophysite missionaries from Egypt and Abyssinia, built monasteries and churches and trading posts in what is now Saudi Arabia as in the other countries we have been thinking about. There were Jewish and Christian communities in places like Mecca and Medina, towns which later in the seventh century became so important for the new faith of Islam. As modern education takes greater hold on modern Saudi Arabia and good universities with various academic disciplines such as archaeology and anthropology are built the Saudi authorities themselves are becoming less defensive concerning their pre-Islamic history and are recognising, albeit somewhat reluctantly, that Islam came not only into a polytheistic society but one in which in different places Judaism and Christianity had flourished for a long time and had clearly influenced the Prophet Muhammad.

The birth and development of the Islamic faith, together with the life of Muhammad, are not our concern here, but it is important that Christians understand these matters if they wish to pray intelligently, and the bibliography at the end of this book will provide suggestions for further reading. The contemporary situation regarding the relationship between Saudi Arabia and Christianity is not a very happy one and is quite different from all that has already been written above; as the Saudi ambassador reminded me, Saudi Arabia is not in any way liberal.

In the eighteenth century CE an Islamic reform movement began in Saudi Arabia which affects the whole of life in the kingdom today, for both Saudi Arabian citizens and expatriates alike, and there are many thousands of Christian expatriates making up an important section of the workforce. This movement, called **Wahha:bism**, is a puritanical movement within Sunni Islam, and it is fundamentally different from, and opposed to, Shia' Islam, as well as to Sufism. Ibn al-Wahha:b travelled a great deal and became disenchanted with much that he saw in Islamic belief and practice. In some ways his 'reformation' within Islam was similar to some elements in the Christian sixteenth century Reformation in Europe; that is, fundamentalist reformers in both religions were opposed to the idea of making pilgrimages to the shrines or supposed burial places of saints and heroes of their respective faiths, a passion for getting back to those fundamentals believed and practised by Jesus of Nazareth and the Prophet Muhammad during their lifetimes, together with a dislike of later teachings, doctrines, interpretations and so on.

Because of the success of Ibn al-Wahha:b, what is now Saudi Arabia became a theocracy and so it continues to this day. Islam is the only recognised religion and Christians may not practise their faith in public and only very discreetly in private; and in any case, not with official approval. It is a very different situation from that found in the other Gulf states, and there are a number of reasons for this. The Kingdom of Saudi Arabia is the homeland of Islam and the cities of Mecca and Medina are the holiest cities for all Muslims, who are required, unless there are very exceptional reasons to prevent them, to make pilgrimage to Mecca at least once in their lifetime and to visit the historic places connected with the life of Muhammad. Christians are strictly banned from visiting these places, but some Muslims take the view that the whole of the province in which Mecca and Medina lie should be banned to non-Muslims; others, even more extreme, believe that the whole Kingdom — as Saudi Arabia is usually called — should exclude non-Muslims. This of course is totally impractical in the modern world and especially in a country which is a world leader in the petro-chemical industry and which depends upon America and western European nations to make huge defence contracts and alliances within it. The non-Muslim workforce in the Kingdom is enormous and without it the Saudi economy would quickly collapse; all of which goes a long way to explain the political and economic enmity towards Saudi Arabia shown by the dissident Saudi exile and Muslim extremist Osama bin Laden.

It is one of the many paradoxes of Middle Eastern life that the really unsettling situations which are a potential danger to Muslims as well as to non-Muslim nations are those in which governments holding extreme religious and secular views are opposed to one another. The revolutionary Shi'ite government of Iran is deeply antagonistic towards Saudi Arabia, believing that the Saudi royal family, who control all the major offices and aspects of Saudi life, has departed from the true Islamic path; and when one begins to look closely into the lifestyle of many well-placed Saudis it is natural to wonder what Ibn al-Wahhab himself would have made of modern Saudi Arabia. There are many Shi'ites in the eastern province of Saudi Arabia who have a tendency to cause trouble for the authorities from time to time. The secularists in countries where the majority of citizens are at least nominally Muslim, such as the Ba'athists of Syria (and formerly Iraq), and the inheritors of the Ataturk revolution in Turkey, have no love for Saudi Arabia. Meanwhile, the Kingdom presents itself to the world as a puritanical Muslim nation maintaining the essentials of the Muslim faith as it perceives them: the strict application of Sharia' law, especially in the carrying out of capital punishment for offences for which most non-Muslims would consider prison sentences adequate. There is a total ban on alcohol and the

The Veil

**O Prophet, direct thy wives and daughters
and the women of the believers
that they should pull down their outer cloaks
from their heads over their faces.
This will make it possible for them
to be distinguished so that they
will not be molested.
Allah is most forgiving, ever merciful.**

al-Quran 33:60
Trans. Muhammad Zafrullah Khan

The covering of the face by a veil has never been universal in the Muslim world. Country women go to the fields without a veil, women in some parts of the Muslim world have not adopted it, others during the last decades have discarded it. But the Quranic injunction to modesty, however it is applied, cannot be set aside. Its interpretation has varied, and does vary, but its importance is basic. One interpretation of what constitutes modesty is the long skirt and head scarf worn by many young women — a stricter interpretation than that of some of their mothers.

Some Muslim women note an obsession among western observers with the question of the veil, an emphasis that tends to trivialise an important debate. The point at issue in the many discussions on the subject of women's role and women's dress is not the veil itself, but the values which Muslim society treasures and seeks to maintain. High among these are honour and good faith, pre-marital chastity and fidelity in marriage. "If the veil still exists, it is because those who are wearing it feel it is part of their tradition and part of their lives", says one woman lawyer.

Charis Waddy[13]

punishments for possessing drugs are severe. Women are not given the respect that the non-Muslim is slowly beginning to show them in terms of equality of opportunity with men in education, in the professions and in politics; women are not permitted to drive vehicles in the Kingdom.

A truly disturbing feature of life in Saudi Arabia is the presence of 'religious police'. These are called **mutawa'i:n** and they have no special qualifications in Muslim theology; they are often students of the **mada:ris**, or religious schools. These (usually) young men are authorised to wander around the streets carrying sticks, to ensure that all people, Muslims and non-Muslims alike, are dressed appropriately according to Muslim standards of dress, and to see that, when the call to prayer begins, especially at dusk, the shops cease to trade until the prayers are concluded. These men make a habit of striking people, and especially women, about the legs and shoulders if they think they are dressed immodestly; all women are expected to wear a head veil and the long black abaya in public and, although non-Muslim women are officially exempt from these rules, many mutawa'i:n overreach themselves in their behaviour towards non-Muslims. These occasions cause near-diplomatic incidents (as when, a few years ago, a group of religious police broke up a children's Christmas party in an international school on the Red Sea coast, causing great distress).

There is an urgent need for the ruling family in Saudi Arabia to set an example of the best in Islamic practice and to provide a real duty of care towards its non-Muslim workforce. All religions have a duty to eradicate from their contemporary value-systems those things that tend to corrupt the original insights of their founders, and this duty is as incumbent upon Islam as it is upon twenty first century Christianity. Part of our praying must at least begin with a resolution to ensure that our private and public practice as Christians is exemplary. We are told that Christians are known as such by the fruits of the Holy Spirit they produce in their daily lives and we can at the very least pray that we and all the children of Abraham — the People of the Book — become repelled by the way in which we exercise a dangerous tendency towards private judgement by interpreting aspects of our faith in ways that suit

**To make factories
and high buildings is easy.
To build man, that is the difficult thing.
Returning to God is an essential way
to achieve the good man
and the good society.**

Mamdouh Mandour[14]

our own predilections, as well as the unpleasant habit religious people have of sitting in judgement on the beliefs and practices of others. Real conversation with God becomes entirely meaningless unless it proceeds from a charitable disposition and, nowadays, abstains from mental and physical cruelty.

In preparing to write *The Muslim Mind* Charis Waddy interviewed many Muslims. In conversation with Abdel Khalek Hassouna, Secretary of the Arab League from 1952 to 1971, she asked a number of questions; the following raises a number of important issues in respect of Saudi Arabia:

Question:
**Islam enjoins fighting a Holy War.
It also promises peace. The Jiha:d in a modern
setting — what is it fought for?
What is it fought against?**

Answer:
**Islam means struggling to ensure freedom
of worship, prevent religious dissension, and
secure the life of humble folk through the
fulfilment of God's commands.
It seeks to communicate the Islamic call to all
people, who are free to take it or leave it.**

See C. Waddy: The Muslim Mind, pp 186–193

**Anyone who kills a human being
shall be put to death...
Anyone who maims another shall suffer
the same injury in return:
fracture for fracture,
eye for eye,
tooth for tooth;
the injury inflicted is the injury
to be suffered.**

Leviticus 24: 17,19–20

You have heard that it was said,
"An eye for an eye and a tooth for a tooth."
But I say to you, Do not resist an evildoer.
But if anyone strikes you on the right cheek,
turn the other also;
and if anyone wants to sue you and take
your coat, give your cloak as well

You have heard that it was said,
"You shall love your neighbour
and hate your enemy".
But I say to you, Love your enemies
and pray for those who persecute you,
so that you may be children of your Father
in heaven.

Matthew 5:38–40, 43–45a

Chapter 9
Human rights and human responsibilities

An illustration of what I am trying to say here in respect of thoughtful prayer is the way in which those of us of the nominally Christian west compare what we perceive as a commitment to human rights to what we consider to be the ignoring of human rights by Muslim states and individual Muslims. We have constantly to remind ourselves not to judge religious practices by their aberrations. Many Muslim states find it difficult to sign up to the United Nations Declaration of Human Rights on the basis that the Universal Islamic Declaration of Human Rights, which dates from 1981, has direct reference to the divine source of all being and to the Quran, which the United Nations Declaration does not have. Christians should perhaps be stronger in affirming that God the creator has given us the right to choose to live in the world in peace and with justice and equity for all, and has given us the ability (but not the right) to choose to ruin everything, including our own lives, and not have a world fit to live in. The lesson of the Garden of Eden is that if we choose the evil path we forfeit the right to live there and we cease to be fully human in the way God intended. This kind of understanding ceases to be merely moralistic when it is applied to the entire solar system, with all the political, economic, environmental, social and demographic issues involved every day; it becomes a matter of life and death, physical and spiritual. Before we as praying Christians begin to demonise Muslim governments for frequently failing to live up to the standards set by their own scholars and legal guides, as in the case, for example, of Saudi Arabia and the Sudan, we need to look into our own failures and those of the so-called Christian states and democracies and begin to work out as people and communities of faith (that is, local congregations) how we may follow Christ actively in establishing conditions of racial tolerance and understanding where we live, safe environments for our children in school and in the streets, in truly caring for all vulnerable people, in ensuring an incorrupt police force and a just and equable legal system. The need for Christians to be pro-active in all these areas is easily recognisable in the United Kingdom, but it is a present need throughout nominally Christian Europe and the Americas. Nor may we easily condemn and feel disgust at the prevalence of the use of torture in Islamic societies so long as clear evidence of its use in so-called Christian communities, as well as by a small number of American and British soldiers in Iraq, continues to emerge.

Democracy – a new religion?

In the years I have spent in the Muslim environment of the Middle East, including the Sudan, I have been told constantly by expatriates, especially those from the west, how much safer they feel walking the streets of the Middle East, day and night, than when they are in their home towns and cities; and I certainly share this view. It is appropriate to be thinking about political and social matters in a book suggesting a fresh approach to prayer. This is because, in the paradoxical way of the modern world, the two Middle Eastern states closest in friendship and political and economic dealings with the United States and Great Britain are Israel and Saudi Arabia; and this strange circumstance does raise huge questions about the way we approach God in prayer.

Since 1991 (the first Gulf war) and more particularly 2001 (the destruction of the New York World Trade Centre), the leaders of the United States and Great Britain have consistently and loudly equated freedom with democracy and have used as opposites tyranny (or terrorism) and dictatorship. They have also quite frequently been close to identifying devout Muslims (those who submit to the will of Allah) with Islamists (radical politicised Muslims). What has been evident for a good many years is a careless use of language of which many of us are guilty; this leads to careless thinking, which is inexcusable and dangerous in people of influence in public office and harmful to self and others in the general public.

Each of the Muslim countries written about in this book is ruled by some form of dictatorship; the rulers themselves are, without exception, paternalistic in the Arab sense of each tribe being looked after by a father, or elder. This is very much a Semitic approach to how a people should be ruled (notwithstanding political Zionism) and there are plenty of precedents in the Old Testament, not least in the stories of Abraham and his descendants. In the Arabian Peninsula most of the rulers began their lives as old-fashioned tribal sheikhs and grew up with a strong sense of a duty of care for their subjects. Most Gulf rulers have, therefore, exercised real paternalistic benevolence in their sheikhdoms and emirates and law and order have been enforced through the **sharia'** courts in accordance with the Quran and the Traditions, and therefore accepted by the people. The effectiveness of this sense of public duty, together with the Quranic enforcement of law, is seen when it is set alongside systems of government in the Middle East where it is not applied, and especially in Iraq under Saddam Hussein, in Syria and in Turkey. In other words, in those Arab and Muslim countries which have become secularised and the forms of religious Islamic rule have been abandoned, there has tended to be a breakdown of law and order in terms of justice and mercy **as the Muslim understands these concepts through the Quran and the Traditions**, and these have been replaced by human rights abuses which Muslim and Christian alike would rightly condemn: torture, imprisonment without trial, summary execution and restriction of basic freedoms.

None of which is to say that Christians can or should agree with or support the Islamic traditions of the more benevolent Arab rulers; but what we can do, and should do as Christians is work actively to eradicate cruelty and injustice wherever it is found, and that certainly includes actively working against cruelty and injustice in western, nominally Christian societies, the so-called democracies, of which there is plenty of evidence: in our prisons, in our inadequate care of the elderly, in our democratic societies that have produced marked divisions between the rich and the poor, the privileged and under-privileged and which have created places such as Guantanamo Bay. Those in power and authority in the Christian world speak as though the democratic principle of rule by those elected by the people is the world's perfect political system. Those who make democracy into some kind of divinity, which is the tendency of the United States of America and of Britain, are in serious danger of exploiting the most outrageous double standards imaginable in affairs of state. This becomes very clear when considering the Kingdom of Saudi Arabia, the West's closest ally in the Middle East and arguably the world's most undemocratic regime. The duty of care for all citizens and visitors that is so important to western democracies is entirely absent from Saudi Arabia. This does not immediately communicate itself to western expatriates secure in their compounds, but begins to be plain when they venture out into the shopping malls of Jeddah, Riyadh and especially the towns of the Eastern Province. Saudi Arabia is ruled by scores of members of the royal family, who employ a religious police force of mutawa'i:n (see chapter 8 above) to enforce Wahha:bism, a form of Islam feared and hated by the majority of Muslims throughout the world and which provides fertile ground for the development of al-Qa'eda and other terrorist organisations, the destruction of which now appears to occupy totally the minds of western leaders. The sycophantic behaviour of the United States and Britain towards Saudi Arabia is actually breeding and indeed encouraging the terrorism we all wish to see defeated and to which end many of the prayers we offer in church are directed. We humans have not yet discovered the perfect system of government which will unite the peoples of the world with their many cultures, religions, political ideologies and sinful ambitions; or, if we have discovered it, we are incapable of putting it into practice. Now, this surely is something for our prayerful reflection leading to action.

Theocracy: the Islamist alternative

Most Arab Muslims, religious or secular, would probably prefer the benevolent paternalistic autocracies under which they live to the western-style democracies they feel are being forced upon them through economic blackmail and military force. When we are thinking about, and praying for, Muslims in the Middle East, we have to consider the real possibility that the ill thought out policies of the western democracies towards Middle Eastern countries are strengthening those elements in Arab, Pakistani and Afghan Islam that are as frightening to moderate

Muslims as they are to Christians. These are the forces within Islam which western leaders call terrorist, forces that I have called Islamist in this book.

Islamists are Muslims who are committed to the ideal of the entire world being ruled by leaders following the teachings of the Prophet Muhammad, the traditions of those who followed him, especially the earliest Imams, and by those Muslims who are authorised to administer sharia' law. They are totally opposed to the democratic ideal and actively discourage British Muslims (for example) from voting in elections. At the same time they oppose the liberal tendencies (as they see them) of most of the Gulf rulers, as well as the Wahha:bism of Saudi Arabia, which they consider has led the Saudis a very long way from pure Islam. Islamists infiltrate the mosques of the western world and encourage young Muslims to leave their homes in America and European countries to travel to special Islamic training centres in countries like Pakistan and the Sudan where they learn to use weapons and prepare themselves for suicide missions. These Islamists are to be found in all countries that have Muslim populations; they assemble under many names, such as Hizbullah (the Party of God), Hizbutahrir (Freedom Party), al-Qa'eda, Hamas and so on. For a clear idea of the Islamists' agenda and on-going plan for Islam in global terms the reader should go to *The Islamist* by Ed Husain (see Some Further Reading, p.137). For our purposes, in trying to think justly about other faiths in order to pray more knowledgeably and more charitably than we do, we should reflect that Islamists may use religious, that is, Islamic, language, but they do not possess hearts and minds that are close to the will of Allah. Their agenda is political and they ignore completely traditional teachings in Islam; for example, the insistence that killing innocent people for whatever reason is a deep offence against Allah, that suicide is forbidden, that the wearing of the veil is a matter of indifference, and so on; they possess a crusading zeal for the restoration of the Caliphate, which was abolished in 1924, to the relief of the vast majority of Muslims. Islamists have a lust for power and control, and little else, as we see clearly when we witness the sectarian violence between Muslims, whipped up by the threatening force of radical Islam; for example, the power struggles between Sunni and Shia' and the cruelty of groups controlled by Islamists towards Christians and other non-Muslims, which is forbidden by the Prophet.

All this is to say that our praying must not contain the thinly-hidden sense that those of us who belong by birth to the western/northern democratically-governed world are the most civilised of peoples; but at the same time we must be acutely aware of the dangers that confront peace-loving people of all faiths, races and cultures and come from those who will do anything to obtain power for themselves. This awareness should compel those of us who belong to democratic nations and are committed Christians also to confront the paradox presented to those who belong to Christ and to the modern free world also; the paradox of belonging to the one who clearly pointed to the imperative of non-violent living and at the same time belonging to nations like America and Britain that unilaterally declare war on nations, such as Iraq, when they think they will. If we do not get our thinking, our understanding and our praying right in these matters that are presented to us every day through the media in our homes, then we shall not have an adequate reply to give to good-living people like Professor Richard Dawkins and other atheists like him who believe deeply that most of the ills in this world have been caused by religions.

Reflection

We might usefully begin this reflection by considering that the greatest threat to all religious faiths, and perhaps especially the three monotheistic faiths in today's world, is secularism, rather than the doctrinal differences between Judaism, Christianity and Islam; and that the strongest secular societies in the Middle East are found in Turkey, Israel and Syria, the first two of which are enthusiastic supporters of British and American secular values. It is arguable that Muslims in Britain and America are far more vocal in their opposition to secularism than are Christians, and that both faiths should be working together to re-discover and publicly affirm those beliefs and values that they have in common.

Seek good and not evil,
that you may live;
and so the Lord, the God of hosts,
will be with you,
just as you have said.
Hate evil and love good,
and establish it in the gate;
it may be that the Lord, the God of hosts,
will be gracious to the remnant of Jacob.

Amos 5:14–15

Happy are those who consider the poor;
the Lord delivers them in the day of trouble.
The Lord protects them and keeps them alive;
they are called happy in the land.

Psalm 41:1–2a

Thus says the Lord:
maintain justice, and do what is right.

Isaiah 56:1

Do not judge,
so that you may not be judged.
For with the judgement you make
you will be judged, and the measure you give
will be the measure you get.
Why do you see the speck in your neighbour's eye,
but do not notice the log in your own eye?
Or how can you say to your neighbour,
"Let me take the speck out of your eye",
while the log is in your own eye?
You hypocrite, first take the log out
of your own eye, and then you will see clearly
to take the speck out of your neighbour's eye.

Matthew 7:1–5

Call to mind when we took a covenant
from the children of Israel:
You shall worship none save Allah,
and shall behave kindly towards parents,
and kindred and the orphans and the needy,
and speak graciously to people
and observe prayer and pay the zakat.
Then you turned away in aversion
except a small number of you.

al–Quran 2:84

**Remind [people] to be subject to rulers
and authorities, to be obedient,
to be ready for every good work,
to speak evil of no one, to avoid quarrelling, to
be gentle, and to show every courtesy
to everyone...**

**those who have come to believe in God
[should] be careful to devote themselves
to good works; these things are excellent and
profitable to everyone.
But avoid stupid controversies, genealogies,
dissensions, and quarrels about the law,
for they are unprofitable and worthless.**

Letter to Titus 3:1–2, 8–9

It is a habit of Christian commentators and writers in this age of Islamic extremism to quote those parts of the Quran that appear to incite violence against Jews and Christians. It is useful, therefore, to our thinking and praying about the Middle East, to reflect on a few verses from the Quran that do the opposite; they also remind us that the agenda of organisations such as al-Qa'eda and the radical Palestinian groups is a political and economic agenda and has little, if any, basis in religious teaching. Through the centuries Jews, Christians and Muslims alike have found it convenient to disguise radical political programmes behind religious texts and vocabulary and much vigilance in thought and prayer is called for. Dialogue between Christians and Muslims at the very least involves trying to understand the scriptures on which their two faiths and value-systems are based and (this is more difficult) trying to decide how far the Christian and Islamic Traditions reflect the minds of their respective founders. Private judgement and interpretation are dangerous paths to follow and this is why for many Christians and Muslims the liturgical community of faith that is called the Church and the Islamic 'umma' which is the spiritual nation that binds Muslims together irrespective of race or nationality, are so important; but their scholars and religious leaders are also under a collective responsibility to guide their faithful adherents towards a greater understanding of their respective faiths, and themselves to ensure that the violent tendencies of the present age, or the secular lifestyle models that eventually lead to these tendencies, do not begin to take over our lives.

People of the Book

**Affirm,
We believe in Allah and in that which has been
sent down to us and that which was sent down
to Abraham and Ishmael and Isaac and Jacob
and his children and that which was given
to Moses and 'Isa, [that is, Jesus] and that
which was given to all the other prophets from
their Lord. We make no distinction between
any of them and to Him do we wholly submit
ourselves.**

al-Quran 2:136–138

**Suicide bombing, hostage taking
and inter-communal strife.**

**O ye who believe, consume not your property
between yourselves unlawfully;
it being lawful to acquire property through
trade with mutual consent;
and destroy not yourselves.
Surely, Allah is ever merciful to you.**

al-Quran 4:30

(Note: Some commentators on the Quran (e.g. Thomas Cleary: The Essential Koran) are a little disingenuous about this verse, and Islamic extremists tend to call suicide bombing 'martyrdom', as something to be encouraged; but Arabic and the Quran have a perfectly good word for 'martyrdom' and 'martyr'. In this verse the Quran seems to be quite clear: **la: taqtulu: anfusakum** means straightforwardly 'do not kill yourselves', and would appear to apply to death by one's own hand in any circumstances (JB).

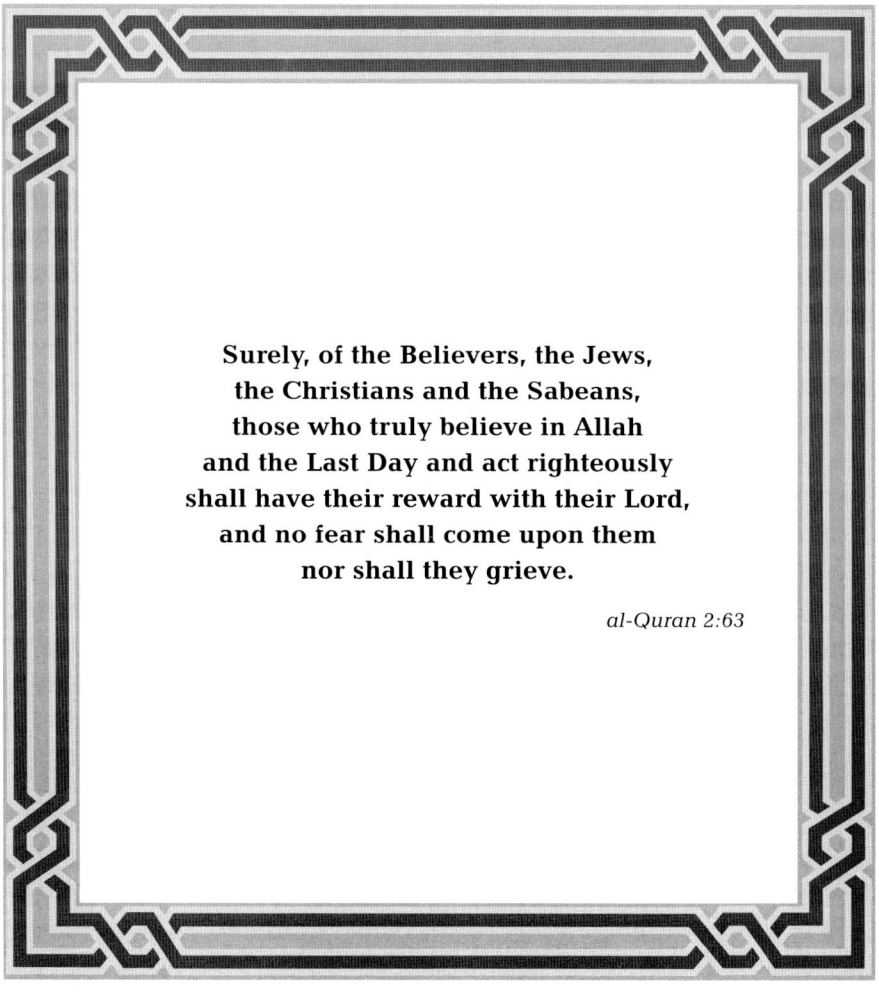

**Surely, of the Believers, the Jews,
the Christians and the Sabeans,
those who truly believe in Allah
and the Last Day and act righteously
shall have their reward with their Lord,
and no fear shall come upon them
nor shall they grieve.**

al-Quran 2:63

**You shall not shed each other's blood,
nor turn your people out of their homes;
thus did you affirm and have throughout
borne witness to it.
Yet you are people who slay one another
and turn out a section of your people
from their homes, backing up their
enemies against them, committing sin and
transgression. Thereafter if they come to
you as captives seeking your help you deem
it meritorious to ransom them, while their
turning out in the first place was unlawful
for you. Do you, then, believe in a part of the
Book and disbelieve in a part of it?**

al-Quran 2:85–87

Finally, is there anything in the following passage to which the Christian could not readily assent, or the sense of which is not echoed in the Bible? The words were spoken by the High Commissioner for Nigeria in London at a Commonwealth service in Westminster Abbey in 1973. They are the opening words of **Surah 57 in the Quran**:

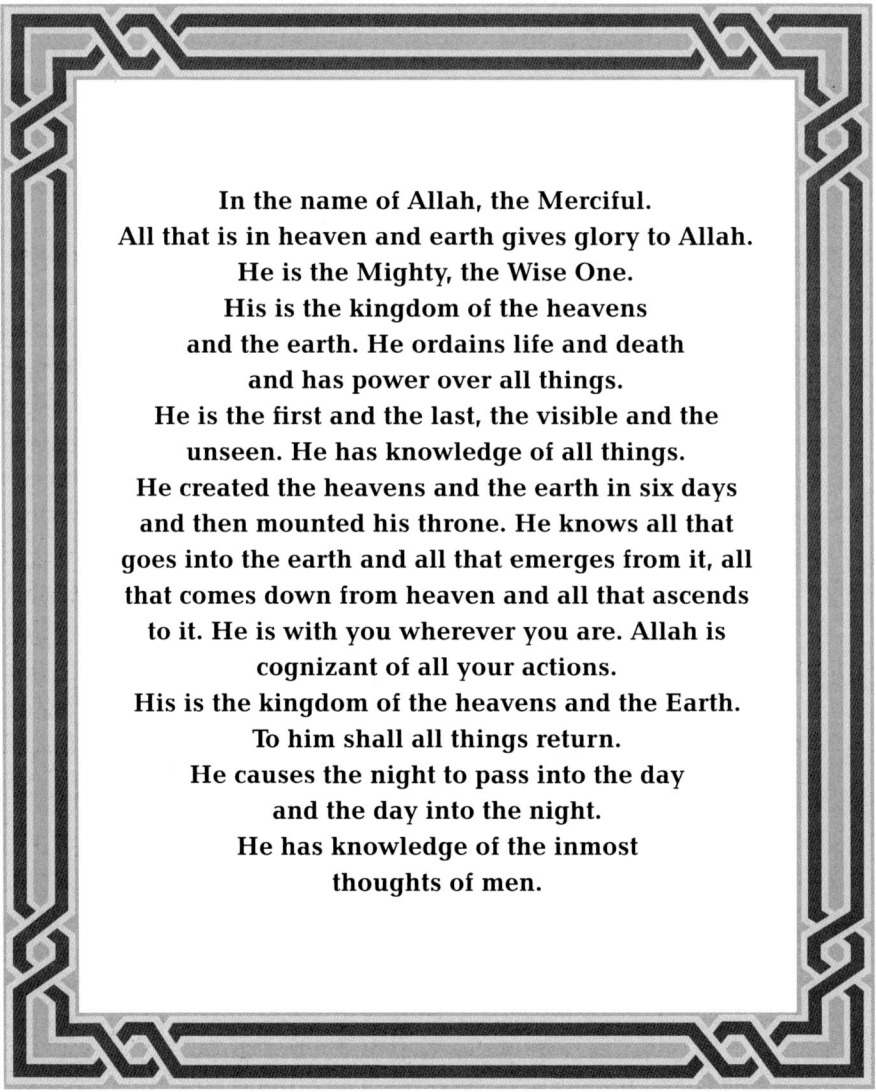

In the name of Allah, the Merciful.
All that is in heaven and earth gives glory to Allah.
He is the Mighty, the Wise One.
His is the kingdom of the heavens
and the earth. He ordains life and death
and has power over all things.
He is the first and the last, the visible and the
unseen. He has knowledge of all things.
He created the heavens and the earth in six days
and then mounted his throne. He knows all that
goes into the earth and all that emerges from it, all
that comes down from heaven and all that ascends
to it. He is with you wherever you are. Allah is
cognizant of all your actions.
His is the kingdom of the heavens and the Earth.
To him shall all things return.
He causes the night to pass into the day
and the day into the night.
He has knowledge of the inmost
thoughts of men.

Kierkegaard wrote:

'The "immediate" person thinks and imagines that when he prays, the important thing, the thing he must concentrate upon, is that God should hear what he is praying for. Yet in the true, eternal sense it is just the reverse: the true relation in prayer is not when God hears what is prayed for, but when the person praying continues to pray until he is the one who hears, who hears what God wills. The "immediate" person, therefore... makes demands in his prayers; the true man of prayer only attends'.[15]

Breathe on me, Breath of God,
fill me with life anew,
that I may love what thou dost love,
and do what thou wouldst do.

Edwin Hatch (1835–1839)
Hymns Ancient & Modern New Standard No.15

Chapter 10
Christian–Muslim Relations
A brief historical overview and a present-day assessment

The 'buzz-word' today, for almost any kind of conversation, is 'dialogue'. I try to remind myself that dialogue is a matter of attitudes and relations as much as words. From the time of the Prophet Muhammad there has always been some kind of interaction between Jews, Christians and Muslims, friendly or otherwise; and, while this book is largely concerned with the relationship between Christians and Muslims, it is important to remember that Muslims are arguably closer to Jews in their basic beliefs and practices than they are to Christians. In pre-Islamic Arabia the Nestorian Christian missionaries did not live in isolation from their pagan neighbours, and the Monophysite Christians from Abyssinia built a great cathedral in Sana'a in Arabia Felix, today's Yemen. As a trader Muhammad travelled the spice and incense routes. The Quran reflects something of his experience of meeting Christians: **You will find the nearest in affection to those who believe** [that is, Muslims] **are those who say, 'We are Christians'. That is because there are among them priests and monks, and because they are not proud.**

Muhammad died in 632 CE and the expansion of Islam out of Arabia into Greater Syria began almost at once. The second Caliph 'Umr captured Jerusalem and refused to receive the surrender of the Patriarch in the Church of the Holy Sepulchre, regarding this place as sacred to Christians. He made a treaty with the Patriarch which states (in part), ['Umr] **grants to the people of Aelia** [that is, Jerusalem] **security of their lives, their possessions, their churches, their crosses... they shall have freedom of religion and none shall be molested unless they rise up in a body. They shall pay a tax instead of military service... and those who leave the city shall be safeguarded until they reach their destination.** I think we need to reflect that the experiences of Muhammad and those of the Patriarch of Jerusalem in dealing with the Muslim invaders, show how wrong and ill-informed many modern Islamists are when they describe Christians as **kuffar** (that is, infidels), and publicly call for their murder.

The interaction of the church and the Muslim community continued while the Muslim conquest took hold. St John of Damascus lived from 675 CE until 753. Christian Damascus surrendered to the Muslims in 635 and until then St John's grandfather was the city's governor. John himself had an Arab name – Mansu:r ibn Sergu:n. Islam seems to have become part of the scenery for Christians, who had 'protected' status on payment of a tax. St John of Damascus was much more concerned in his writings with Christian heresies rather than with Muslim beliefs and from the seventh century on for many centuries Christians were an important part of the civil administrations of Muslim cities and regions. Christian writings began to be translated into Arabic and when in the eighth century the Nestorian Patriarch Timothy I moved the headquarters of his church from Ctesiphon to Baghdad he met regularly with the Caliph.

During the years of the Muslim conquest and the settlement of Muslims (armies and Arab administrators) in lands that had been mixed polytheistic, Jewish and Christian, the meeting of Christian and Muslim minds was chiefly in the areas of Greater Syria and Baghdad. The churches in the countries bordering the Mediterranean were almost silent after the seventh century, apart from Egypt, which retained its strong apostolic traditions and the Coptic influence.

After the conquest of Spain Christians were protected and paid the tax and many Christians, especially the young, came under the spell of Arab learning and social customs; a letter written in 854 CE by one Alvaro speaks of young Spaniards being "intoxicated with Arab eloquence". Occasionally, however, there was trouble and in Cordobà in the ninth century Christians were executed for supposedly insulting the Prophet and rioting followed.

Through the centuries of the Middle Ages Christians were having perforce to learn to live at peace with their conquerors if they were to survive mentally and physically. In the tenth century Greeks from the mainland went to Cyprus and massacred many Muslims. A Muslim expeditionary force reacted and took Cypriot Christians as slaves to Baghdad. This sad episode resulted in correspondence between Patriarch Nicholas I and the Caliph of Baghdad in an attempt to reach a settlement.

After the early centuries of Islam attempts to establish good relationships between Christians and Muslims became a non-priority as politics took over and, as always happens between people who hold strong convictions, internal quarrelling began between Muslims. The **Fatimids** of Egypt had expansionist ambitions and destroyed the Church of the Holy Sepulchre in 1010 CE. The **Seljuks** [Turks] invaded Mesopotamia and much reduced the influence of the **Ummayads**. The Byzantine Christians had ambitions to take advantage of these divisions within Islam, but at that point Western Christendom began to look eastwards, with militant expansionist ambitions not only to recapture the Holy Land for the Latin Christians but also to assert the superiority and authority of Latin Christendom over Byzantium. So in many ways the **Crusades**, about which Arab Muslims still get very animated and agitated, were as much about western Christianity's enmity towards Byzantine Christianity and Constantinople as about Arab Islam and Jerusalem; it has to be said also that there is not much to choose between the war-lords who led the Crusades, such as King Richard I of England and Guy de Lusignan of France and the Christian war-lords who caused such terror in Lebanon and Beirut in the 1980s.

Between the tenth and twelfth centuries there was plenty of interaction between Christian and Muslim academics in the universities of Europe; within Christianity this involved, for example, the Benedictine abbey of Cluny in southern Burgundy where the Quran was translated into Latin during the time when Peter the Venerable was abbot. The Dominicans were active in this field, especially in the work of St Thomas Aquinas; also the Franciscans with St Francis of Assisi himself and Raymond Lull. The Christians were influenced a great deal by the work of Muslim scholars in interpreting classical texts, and especially Aristotle; this was particularly important to the western Latin church, whose teaching had been dominated until the Middle Ages by St Augustine. Muslim scholars such as Avicenna (Ibn Sina) of Bokhara (980–1037 CE), al-Ghazali the Persian theologian and philosopher (1058–1111 CE) and Averroes (Ibn Rushd) of Cordobà in Spain (1126–1198) brought a fresh look not only to Christianity as a result of the translation of their works into Latin and Hebrew, but also to orthodox Sunni Islam, because their thinking (and they did not always agree with one another) in the fields of philosophy, law, medicine and theology questioned many of the presuppositions of traditional Islam. Altogether, this interaction between Muslim and Christian scholars, through their published works and across three centuries, changed the academic character and thinking within both Islam and Christianity for many centuries to come.

From the sixteenth century the Christian church in the west was in turmoil on many fronts and dialogue with Islam was very much a secondary issue almost into the twentieth century. The Reformation and Counter-Reformation brought about a deep reappraisal of Christian doctrine and practice from within and maybe, had the theologians of the day not been too preoccupied to think about it, it would have been noted that the question of salvation through faith by the grace of God, together with the place of good works in both church and society, has a direct bearing on important points of difference between Christianity and Islam.

On the political front Spain and Europe as a whole were freed from Muslim domination and the power of the Ottoman Empire was diminished. As the political ambitions of western European nations began to spread along the southern shores of the Mediterranean and into the Levant, Christian missions, both Catholic and Protestant, sprang up. It was almost as if the turmoil of the 16th century had caused Christians to become particularly aggressive towards those who did not agree with them and it was not until towards the end of the 19th century that missionaries in Muslim lands, in the Middle East and southwards into Africa, combined a real desire for converts to the faith of Jesus Christ with a more explicit humanitarian approach that led to the establishment of excellent Christian schools and colleges and the emergence of missionaries who acquired, on the job as it were, a thorough academic and practical knowledge of Arabic and Islam. Christian–Muslim dialogue became a reality once more, in the universities, colleges and in the work-place, and this, in the later nineteenth and early twentieth centuries, laid the foundation for the great revolution in theological, political, economic and social thinking after World War I.

Christian–Muslim Dialogue today

It was almost as if, after the restrictions of war and the realisation that our hold on life is a very fragile thing, people throughout the world felt emancipated from whatever it was that had held them in thrall and they embarked on radical new and revolutionary ways of thinking and acting. The long centuries of Ottoman rule were ended at a stroke by Kamal Ataturk the founder of secular Turkey, and the Caliphate was abolished in 1924. In the Middle East promises were made, only to be broken at Versailles in the carve up of the lands east of the Mediterranean between Britain, France and the Hashemite dynasty; the Balfour Declaration of 1917 set in motion the process that culminated in the establishment of the State of Israel in 1947, a process which also led to the bitter enmity in Israel/Palestine between Jews and Arabs, both Christian and Muslim. The economic and social revolution was accelerated by the discovery of oil in the Arabian Peninsula between the two World Wars. The Gulf sheikhs quickly understood that they could not develop any of this new resource without western technology and, for a good many years, western expertise to apply it. The world of Gertude Bell, Freya Stark and Wilfred Thesiger quickly began to disappear and many thousands of skilled and unskilled expatriates were brought into the Gulf to service this new revolution: doctors, nurses, teachers, technocrats, bankers and commercial entrepreneurs from the west but chiefly from the Indian sub-continent, Sri Lanka, the Philippines, Korea, the Sudan, Palestine and Egypt, with the result that the Arabian Peninsula became a rich mixture of Muslim, Christian, Hindu and Buddhist.

All this, and much more, meant that the relationship between Christian and Muslim in the Arab Middle East ceased to be confined to the academic sphere and diplomacy, and extended into the world of commerce and industry as well as into the educational sphere at pre-university level. In the Middle East western technocrats, bankers, teachers and hospital staff became very familiar with the cycle of everyday Muslim life: the daily times of prayer, the Muslim festivals, the strong discipline of faith in practice during the month of Ramadan and so on. These matters were not simply things that happened to interrupt daily routine; they were matters to be enquired about and discussed over mid-morning coffee and staff room meetings. At the same time Christians in the Middle East are generally not so reluctant, whether they are regular churchgoers or not, to hide the fact that they are Christians. In any case western Christians are in a minority in the workplaces of the Arabian Peninsula and Asian Christians are not shy about speaking of their faith in Jesus Christ. So, in Middle Eastern situations where Christians are a small minority of the total population and live and work, not only among their Muslim colleagues, but alongside hundreds of expatriate Hindus and Buddhists, Christian–Muslim dialogue becomes part of daily living and there are many opportunities for people of different faiths to speak of their beliefs and religious practices; joining in conversation also brings the challenge to Christians and others alike to understand their own faith and value systems better.

It is important, while all this is going on, that Christians who are not indigenous to the Middle East should not allow themselves to be carried away with the kind of enthusiasm that would lay them open to charges of syncretism. All religions are not the same and Islam and Christianity differ widely on some of the central tenets of Christian faith, such as the reality and meaning of the Person of Christ and of his death on the cross. Middle Eastern Arab Christians, apart from academics, are generally reluctant to engage Muslims in any kind of religious discussion or debate. Many Arab Christians have had bad experiences in modern times at the hands of militant Islam; for example, in Algeria, in Upper Egypt, and especially in Iraq, where the Chaldean Christians, who have been in Mesopotamia almost since the beginning of the Christian era, are being systematically killed or forced into exile by the Muslim warlords and power hungry insurgents. This is no way ignores or diminishes the horror of the mass killing of Bosnian Muslims by Serb Christians (for example), but all these events do go to show how many of the actions of militant western powers can in themselves destroy the human rights of millions of people, and especially the basic human right to worship God according to one's conscience and without fear of persecution. It is not too surprising that so many Christians and Muslims are wary of engaging in dialogue with one another.

This book has been written in an attempt chiefly to help Christians who are not resident in the Middle East, and especially the Arabian Peninsula, to pray with more knowledge and sensitivity about Christian–Muslim relationships as they tend to be in these violent times and as they should be in settled times. But what of the attitudes of Christians in today's United Kingdom and for that matter in the United States? A great deal of effort needs to be put in to the business of daily living in multi-faith societies where the two big issues of immigration and homophobia result in considerable unrest, within those societies themselves and, almost more seriously, deep within the human psyche. A good example of the way in which local churches can inspire local communities to be more responsible in their thinking about multi-faith matters, and more caring in their practices, is to be found in the establishment of the Christian–Muslim Forum founded in 2006, after some years of careful preparatory work and of which the Archbishop of Canterbury is the Founding Patron. The Report, entitled *Presence and Engagement*, which was prepared for the Archbishop's Council of the Church of England is, to my mind, noteworthy for its practicality and markedly different from the scores of academic and theoretical reports which, however useful, have been produced over many years. It invites churches to consider their lifestyle in a diverse religious, ethnic and cultural society, whether they are equipped to deal with rapid change and in what ways they can work ecumenically in cooperation with people of other faiths. These considerations are crucial for Christians who, according to their own differing traditions, have various attitudes regarding the understanding of the Christian message. For example, Christians living in a multi-faith society should ask precisely how they relate the New Testament teaching about salvation through faith in Jesus Christ, or about Jesus as Son of God, to the beliefs and prayers of those among us who declare with all their hearts and minds: **God is great; there is no God but God and Muhammad is the prophet of God.** Are Christians able to live with this, or do they feel obliged (by God perhaps?) actively to proclaim the Christian gospel to Muslims with a view to their conversion? What is forbidden in the Middle East may be possible, and certainly allowable, in Britain or America. At the same time we may remember that Muslims are committed by their faith to seek converts and Islam is a religion with a global outreach.

I began this chapter by reflecting that dialogue is as much a matter of attitudes and relations as of words. My own belief is that Christianity and Islam can never agree on doctrinal matters of religious belief, any more than Christians and Jews can. Our doctrines and beliefs regarding the Fatherhood of God, Original Sin, the understanding of the Promised Land, the calling and sending of the Messiah, the Christian understanding of the Crucifixion of Jesus of Nazareth and redemptive sacrifice, the meaning of the Holy Trinity, and many others, have caused the Children of Abraham, the People of the Book, to go into the wilderness that is this world along different routes; and if the world is to survive the horrors that sinful human beings have inflicted and are inflicting on themselves and others, then the only way forward is surely for human beings together to find a way in and through the wilderness.

If what I have said above is true, and that there is no likelihood that Jews, Christians and Muslims can ever agree on matters of belief and doctrine, then our three ways through the wilderness have to converge in such a way that our common humanity will discover the ways, together with people of other faiths and of no faith, in which the best and highest values may triumph over the basest. As the Report for the Archbishops' Council is entitled, all this calls for Presence and Engagement, and this calling is primarily that of those of us who live as faithful Christians in our communities and attend our local churches.

Presence refers to the Christian imperative to be Christ in our communities to all others, irrespective of race, colour or creed: the good, the wicked and the indifferent. Now this has nothing to do with being politically correct, it is not setting out a social or political programme; it is the gospel, the good news for humanity proclaimed by Jesus of Nazareth and lived out by him in a way that we can follow, by an active faith. One of the great examples of someone who lived out the Christian presence in his life was Charles de Foucauld. A French cavalry officer in the last quarter of the nineteenth century, Charles turned to Christ, was ordained as a priest and eventually became a hermit deep in the hinterland of the Sahara desert, in today's Algeria. He faithfully said Mass day by day in his hermitage and was loved as a holy man by the local tribesmen. As far as is known no Muslim became a Christian as a result of Charles de Foucauld's ministry in the desert, but his presence as a faithful Christian among Muslims was welcomed and it is clear that in the manner of his life he influenced many Christians (chiefly French soldiers in the desert forts) and Muslims for good. It is one of the paradoxes of the Christian vocation that in 1916 this holy man was assassinated, possibly a victim of a local jiha:d. We may think that it is impossible to live such a life as Charles de Foucauld lived, and that may be true with regard to his extreme austerity; but we should concentrate on Christ's need for us to declare his presence in the world by being Christ in our local communities, by our persistent and prayerful faith and, as Brother Roger of Taizé was always joyfully proclaiming, living out the life of the Beatitudes (Matthew 5:1–16). If we are able by God's grace to be the living Christian presence in our local communities of faith as well as in our personal lives, then we shall surely be able, by the same amazing grace, to engage in many important ways, not only with those who are of the same mind as ourselves, but with those who are closest to the heart and mind of God as seen in the person and work of Jesus Christ. It is at this point that we can begin to reflect that the person and work of Jesus Christ is all-embracing, non-discriminatory, reaching out with God's love to the most disadvantaged, the totally destitute, the most abandoned, the most unloved. When as Christians we are able to grasp in our daily lives that all this is at the heart of the Good News, when we are equipped not only to believe it but to live it, then in our multi-faith communities we shall be happily surprised to discover that people who believe and live sincerely with the teachings of other faiths, like devout Muslims, will be keen to engage in what is surely the vocation of all those who profess to believe in God, to work to fulfil God's will for all humanity to live in peace and harmony and with justice with one another. Many initiatives leading to real and important advances in good relationships between Christians and people of other faiths are taking place on international, national and local levels throughout Europe, the Middle East and America; and yet our communities of faith, whether Jewish, Christian, Muslim or other faiths, are still beset by many deep-rooted fears and misunderstandings that even reach into the highest levels of government and legislation. This book has been written to try to dispel some of the ignorance that results in Islamophobia within local church communities and it recognises that much hard work at a mental, spiritual and practical level needs to be done before we who are Christian can claim to live in communities that are entirely liberated from fear of those who are different from ourselves in race, colour, social customs and religious belief. In Britain many church and civic communities have begun to take important steps to build a better environment for children and the elderly, as is seen in much that is described in the Report *Presence and Engagement.* There is a growing recognition that engagement with Muslims, for example, does not in any sense require, by either a Christian or a Muslim, a watering down of deeply held religious convictions or making a compromise over doctrines. Christians and Muslims may bring to a fruitful relationship what is best in each faith and those things that are held in common, in order to achieve more harmonious living. In Britain Christians and Muslims alike have a deep concern for the way our schools and hospitals are managed. The debate about Faith-schools is only just beginning and the discussion concerning children's dress in schools has hardly been settled; the same may be said concerning the wearing of the veil in the workplace. Church schools, Voluntary Aided and Controlled, should be able to initiate non-confrontational discussions with regard to such matters, as well as the consideration of whether Christian and Muslim children should be given religious education in one another's faith systems, and by qualified teachers who do not have a proselytising agenda; it is at least arguable that it is a poor society that is unable to contemplate such possibilities. In business, employers and managers should be fully conversant with the customs of, say, a Muslim or Sikh employee and able to engage in the kind of dialogue that will build industrial relations. In medical contexts it would be valuable for Jews, Christians, Muslims and members of other faiths to have some understanding of one another's value systems regarding birth control, abortion, the management of the last days of life for children and adults and other things touching on the meaning of human creation and destiny in the three monotheistic religions. Reports come in from many parts of Britain showing that attitudes towards other faiths are changing, however slowly, and relationships between people who gather to worship according to their own traditions are growing closer and warmer all the time. This welcome process can only be helped along by Christians, Muslims, Sikhs, Hindus and Buddhists understanding their own faiths more thoroughly. To be in the presence of God in public worship and private devotion and through that close relationship with God to be engaged in building up good reconciling inter-faith relationships is to make a loving response in a messy and violent world to the love of God which is for ever trying to break through into the whole of creation.

Soon after I left my full-time work as bishop of Cyprus and the Gulf I was invited to take part in a Jewish-Christian-Muslim dialogue on the theme of "Religion and Violence; Religion and Peace". The meeting took place over several days in the Centre for Dialogue and Prayer opposite the gates of the Auschwitz-Birkenau death camp. The participants included rabbis, priests and Muslim scholars, as well as lay scholars; among them were chief rabbis, several cardinals and a number of leading muftis. Lectures were delivered and discussed and new friendships were formed, but before we all left we spent several hours together in the two former concentration camps. As we walked through the Birkenau gate with its infamous title "Work makes you free" and along the railway track that carried thousands of Jews and Gentiles to the gas chambers there was very little conversation. We arrived at the memorial garden and listened to readings from Jewish scriptures. Then, with great spontaneity, Jews, Christians and Muslims began to pray, chiefly in Hebrew and Arabic.

Here, then, is a paradigm of what this book has been about: Jews, Christians and Muslims walking together, even through disastrous and horrific historical circumstances, often in silence and, in the silence, offering up our own individual, communal and national hatreds, xenophobia and anxieties, together with our aspirations and deepest longings for peace and tranquillity, to the One and only Almighty God who sent Abraham and his family on their journey of faith.

Jews, Muslims and Christians walking along the railway line that led to Auschwitz-Birkenau where they prayed together.

**There is no such thing as a holy war
in Christianity, nor in Islam,
nor in Judaism. Only peace is holy,
for peace is the name of God.**

*Ref: Midrash Rabba on Leviticus 9:9
quoted by Rabbi René-Samuel Sirat
Chief Rabbi Emeritus of Europe,
at the Auschwitz conference.*

**Surely those who have faith
in this divine writ,
as well as those who follow the Jewish faith,
and the Christians and the Sabians,
all who believe in God and the Last Day
and do righteous deeds shall have their reward
with their Lord, and no fear need they have,
and neither shall they grieve.**

al-Quran 2:62

Love your enemies,
do good to those who hate you,
bless those who curse you,
pray for those who abuse you.
If anyone strikes you on the cheek,
offer the other also;
and from anyone who takes away your coat
do not withold even your shirt...
Do to others as you would have them
do to you...
Love your enemies, do good,
and lend, expecting nothing in return.
Your reward will be great,
and you will be the children of the Most High;
for he is kind to the ungrateful
and the wicked. Be merciful,
just as your father is merciful.

*Gospel according to St Luke,
Ch 6, verses 27–36 (parts)*

Notes

1. Fisk, R.
   Pity the Nation. (OUP 1990) Chapter 11 "Terrorists".
2. Eaton, J.
   The Psalms: See commentary on Psalm 137; pages 454–456.
3. Rassam, S.
   Christianity in Iraq. (Gracewing 2005).
4. *Waddy, C.*
   The Muslim Mind 2nd edition (1982. Longman). Pages 101–102.
5. See Suleiman, Khalid A (ed)
   Palestine and Modern Arab Poetry. (Zed Books 1984). Pages 116–117.
6. See Abdullah al-Udhari (trans)
   Victims of a Map. (Al Saqi Books, Zed Press 1984). Pages 62–63.
7. C. Waddy.
   The Muslim Mind, page 122.
8. *The Muslim Mind*, page 41: "Minorities".
9. S Rassam.
   Christianity in Iraq, Chapter 7.
10. Bishop Kenneth Cragg.
    Having in Remembrance: a calendar of Middle East saints.
    Entry July 15th.
11. Tim Mackintosh Smith.
    Yemen: Travels in a Dictionary Land, page 238.
12. See John Eaton.
    The Psalms p 446.
13. C. Waddy.
    The Muslim Mind p 65.
14. See C. Waddy.
    The Muslim Mind p 13.
    Mandouh Mandour, ex-President Cairo University Student Union.
15. Bishop George Appleton (Ed.)
    The Oxford Book of Prayer (OUP 1985) page 259.

Some Further Reading

The literature on Middle Eastern topics is vast and new material appears most weeks. However, most of the books mentioned here are of a general, non-specialist nature and should give the reader suffficient material to feed further interest in, and knowledge of, the region and the faith systems within it.

Algosaibi, Ghazi A. *The Gulf Crisis.* (Kegan Paul 1993).

Allen, Mark. *Arabs.* (Continuum 2006).

Al-Qasimi, Sultan Muhammad.
The Myth of Arab Piracy in the Gulf. (Routledge 2nd ed. 1988).

Al-mu'mini:n, Amir (ed). *Supplications (Muslim prayers).*
(The Muhammadi Trust).

Al-Udhari, Abdullah (trans.) *Victims of a Map.* (Al Saqi Books (Zed) 1984). This is a bi-lingual anthology of Arabic poetry.

Asad, Muhammad. *The Road to Mecca.* (The Muslim Academic Trust 1998).

Betts, Robert B. *Christians in the Arab East.* (SPCK 1979).

Bin Talal, Hassan. *Search for Peace.* (MacMillan 1984).

Bulloch, John. *The Gulf.* (Century Publishing 1984).

Cleary, Thomas. *The Essential Koran. (Readings from the Qur'an).*
(Harper San Francisco 1993).

Cragg, Kenneth. *Sandals at the Mosque.* (SCM Press 1959 1st edition).

Cragg, Kenneth. *Jesus and the Muslim.* (Allen & Unwin 1985).

Cragg, Kenneth. *The Arab Christian.* (Westminster\John Knox 1991).

Dagher, Carole H. *Bring Down the Walls. (Lebanon's Post-war challenge)*
(St Martin's Press 2000).

Dalrymple, William. *From the Holy Mountain.* (Harper Collins / Flamingo 1997).

Denffer, Ahmad Von. *'Ulu:m al-Qur'an: an introduction to the Sciences of the Qur'an.* (The Islamic Foundation 1983).

Ellis, Marc H. *Towards a Jewish Theology of Liberation.* (SCM Press 1987).

Fisk, Robert. *Pity the Nation.* (OUP 1990).

Fisk, Robert. *The Great War for Civilisation: the conquest of the Middle East.* (Harper Perennial Revised ed. 2006).

Fitzgerald, Michael L and John Borelli. *Interfaith Dialogue: A Catholic View.* (SPCK 2006).

Gardner, Frank. *Blood and Sand.* (Bantam 2007).

Guillaume, A. *Islam.* (Penguin Books 1954).

Husain, Ed. *The Islamist.* (Penguin Books 2007).

Hussein, Kamal. *City of Wrong.* (Geoffrey Bles 1959).

Laqueur, W and Barry Rubin. *The Israeli-Arab Reader: a documentary history of the Middle East conflict.* (Penguin Books 6th revised ed. 2001).

Lings, Martin. *Muhammad.* (Islamic Texts Society 1998).

Mackintosh-Smith, Tim. *Yemen: Travels in a Dictionary Land.* (John Murray 1997).

Mansfield, Peter. *The Arabs.* (Penguin 1990).

Moon, James S. *Sweetman's Islam and Christian Theology.* (Centre for the Study of Islam and Christian-Muslim Relations, Selly Oak).

Nazir-Ali, Michael. *Islam: a Christian Perspective.* (Paternoster Press 1983).

Rantisi, Audeh and Pat. *Blessed Are the Peacemakers.* (Eagle 2003).

Rassam, Suha. *Christianity in Iraq.* (Gracewing 2005).

Simpson, John. *The Wars Against Saddam.* (MacMillan 2003).

Simpson, John. *From the House of War.* (Arrow Books 1991).

Sulaiman, Khalid A. *Palestine and Modern Arab Poetry.* (Zed Books 1984).

Waddy, Charis (ed). *The Muslim Mind. Longman 2nd edition 1982.*

Watt, W Montgomery. *The Formative Period of Islamic Thought.* (Edinburgh University Press 1973. One World Press edition 1998).

About Christians Aware

Christians Aware is an international and interdenominational educational charity working to develop multi-cultural and inter faith understanding and friendship locally, nationally and internationally.
Its aim is to work for justice, peace and development. The focus is on listening to encourage awareness and action.

It does this with a programme of focus groups, conferences, international exchanges, work-camps and publications. *Travel with Awareness* is a book of guidance for the international visits which are often to places where there are or have been situations of conflict, such as Palestine, Israel and Rwanda. Groups also visit places where there are acute development needs, including primary health care, education and water harvesting.

The words of Ronald Wynne are important:

'Do not try to teach anyone anything until you have learnt something from them.'